Men-at-Arms • 490

Imperial German Colonial and Overseas Troops 1885–1918

Alejandro de Quesada . Illustrated by Stephen Walsh

Series editor Martin Windrow

First published in Great Britain in 2013 by Osprey Publishing, Midland House, West Way, Botley, Oxford, OX2 0PH, UK

43–01 21st Street, Suite 220B, Long Island City, NY 11101, USA

E-mail: info@ospreypublishing.com

OSPREY PUBLISHING IS PART OF THE OSPREY GROUP

A CIP catalog record for this book is available from the British Library

Print ISBN: 978 1 78096164 4
PDF e-book ISBN: 978 1 78096 165 1
ePub e-book ISBN: 978 1 78096 166 8

Editor: Martin Windrow
Index by Zoe Ross
Typeset in Helvetica Neue and ITC New Baskerville
Originated by PDQ Media, Bungay, UK
Printed in China through Worldprint Ltd

13 14 15 16 17 10 9 8 7 6 5 4 3 2 1

Osprey Publishing is supporting the Woodland Trust, the UK's leading woodland conservation charity, by funding the dedication of trees.

www.ospreypublishing.com

Author's Note

Writing a complete history of Imperial Germany's colonial and overseas troops would be a voluminous project, and this work is intended simply as a primer for those seeking a basic understanding of the subject. Some aspects are, inevitably, treated only briefly; the Osprey publications shown on the inside back cover are recommended as companions to this work.

Acknowledgments

The author would like to thank the following individuals, societies, and archives for their assistance and support:
Thomas Brackmann, Phillip Buhler, Chris Dale, Malcolm Fisher, and Malcolm Gordon.
Imperial War Museum, London; The Company of Military Historians, USA; South African National Museum of Military History, Johannesburg; Militärhistorischen Museum der Bundeswehr, Dresden; Alte Feste Museum, Windhoek, Namibia; Kolmannskop Ghost Town, Namibia; Lüderitz Museum, Namibia; Tsumeb Museum, Namibia; Sam Cohen Library, Swakopmund, Namibia; Swakopmund Museum, Namibia; Der Traditionsverband ehemaliger Schutz- und Überseetruppen – Freunde der früheren deutschen Schutzgebiete e. V.; and AdeQ Historical Archives.

Artist's Note

Readers may care to note that the original paintings from which the color plates in this book were prepared are available for private sale. All reproduction copyright whatsoever is retained by the Publishers. All enquiries should be addressed to:

http://www.stephenwalshillustrations.co.uk/

The Publishers regret that they can enter into no correspondence upon this matter.

OPPOSITE **Portrait of a Schutztruppe major serving in German Southwest Africa. He is wearing the khaki cotton hot-weather uniform, as prescribed (with cornflower-blue piping for all colonies) in November 1896 and used well into World War I. All patterns of the privately purchased uniforms authorized for officers and senior NCOs might vary in such details as collars and pockets, and officers enjoyed latitude in their choice of headgear. Among the medal ribbons displayed on this deep bar is that for the 1904–08 Southwest Africa campaign – see Plate H7. (AdeQ HA)**

IMPERIAL GERMAN COLONIAL AND OVERSEAS TROOPS 1885–1918

GERMANY'S EMERGENCE AS A COLONIAL POWER

The Prussian-led victory over France in 1871 was accompanied by the unification of the many German states into the German Empire under the Prussian throne. This Reich was technically a federation of four kingdoms (Prussia, Bavaria, Saxony, and Württemberg), plus 21 duchies, principalities, and minor states. The Prussian architect of this long-planned project, Otto von Bismarck, was rewarded with appointment as Imperial Germany's first chancellor (prime minister), and continued to dominate her domestic political affairs and foreign policy during the reign of the first emperor, Kaiser Wilhelm I (r.1871–88).

German missionaries and traders had established footholds in various regions earlier in the 19th century, and on June 23, 1884 Bismarck announced a policy of colonial annexation by proxy: charters would be granted to commercial enterprises to negotiate "protectorates" – i.e., they would acquire rights over various territories, under guarantees of Imperial protection. Several protectorates were established in Africa and the Pacific, each with its resident Imperial commissioner (Reichs-Kommissar).

After the accession of the Kaiser's volatile younger son as Wilhelm II (r.1888–1918), Germany became more strident in its demands for recognition as an equal by the older European colonial powers. Bismarck overplayed his political hand at home, and in 1890 the Kaiser dismissed this cautious counselor. German trading companies penetrated ever deeper into non-European markets; a surge of assertive patriotism saw the creation of organizations such

as the Pan-German League, the Colonial League, and the Navy League, and powerful industrialists and businessmen began to exert heavy influence over the German government. The inadequate colonial administrations provided by the original trading companies soon saw the protectorates transformed into crown colonies, ruled by governors appointed by a Colonial Office in Berlin.

Meanwhile, the Imperial General Staff became a power-center in Wilhelm II's highly militaristic regime, and was released from civilian political control. By the outbreak of World War I in August 1914, significant elements of German public opinion were motivated by a belief that other nations were preventing Germany from assuming its rightful place as a world power. In the event, the Great War that ensued would see the extinction of Germany's colonies when they were barely a generation old.

Dr Georg Irmer began his activities in the trading conglomerate Deutsche Kolonialgesellschaft (German Colonial Company), but joined the Colonial Office in 1892. This portrait dates from between December 1893 and March 1898, when he served as Landeshauptmann (colonial administrator) of the Marshall Islands; in 1899–1900 he worked at the head office of the Colonial Service in Berlin, and later as a consular official in Italy and Australia. (AdeQ HA)

* * *

During the 1880s, German colonial activity in Africa followed the usual process of "bribe, divide, expand, exploit, and rule." Given the fragmented nature of these societies, the initial negotiation of protectorates with the often eager chiefs of individual coastal tribes was carried out by the government-chartered companies, which concluded commercial treaties but also raised the Imperial flag. (In most cases these chiefs had no conception of the individual "ownership" of territory in the European sense.)

The German traders usually recruited a few local auxiliaries, and the new Imperial commissioners raised larger police units to quell any unrest generated by the colonizers' activities. As holdings expanded during the 1890s, and protectorates became colonies, these police were supplemented with "defense troops" (Schutztruppe), under the control not of the Army but of the Colonial Office, to which each colony's garrison answered separately. These troops, too, were almost invariably recruited locally or from nearby territories, under cadres of German officers and senior NCOs.

The steady expansion of German holdings meant that for 20-odd years there was almost continuous fighting in one or other of the colonies, as small columns of German-led troops imposed their control over populations scattered throughout often vast regions of rugged terrain. These conflicts ranged from minor skirmishes to bloody campaigns, and there is space in this book to mention only the most important. (For simplicity, we use the conventional term "rebellions;" in fact, many were actually wars of resistance, since they were fought by peoples who had never recognized German authority.)

In parallel, German expansion involved Berlin in constant diplomacy, while the European powers then engaged in the "scramble for Africa" wrangled over, and eventually agreed, mutual boundaries of activity. By 1911 this cynical international horse-trading had finally won Germany a free hand in her areas of interest.

The colonial Schutztruppe

The actual German presence in her colonies varied widely. For instance, between 1902 and 1914 German civilian settlement in Deutsch-Südwest Afrika rose from about 2,600 to 11,600 people, but in 1913 little Togo had a German population of just 316.

In parallel, the Schutztruppen were one of the smallest colonial military organizations in the world, with a combined strength in 1900 of some 3,000 officers and men. While the total temporary forces in Southwest Africa during the Herero Rebellion (1904–07) exceeded 17,000 men, by 1914 the Schutztruppen in all the colonies combined numbered just 6,461 of all ranks. Of these, 14 company-sized units were stationed in German East Africa, 12 companies in Cameroon, and 9 companies in German Southwest Africa (Togo did not have a Schutztruppe, but only a paramilitary police force).

The Schutztruppe in each colony was led by officer and NCO volunteers from the Imperial Army and Navy, and in Southwest Africa – where relations between the colonizers and the indigenous population were the most hostile – the rank and file were also German. Despite the dangers of combat and disease, such postings were popular among adventurous soldiers bored by the rigid routines of home service, and the pay rates were attractive.

The local African rank and file, termed *askaris*, usually enlisted for an initial five-year term that could be extended in increments. High standards of discipline and marksmanship were demanded and achieved, and the askaris earned a reputation for loyalty. The company was the tactical unit, and field training was carried out at that level; initially African troops were issued with 11mm Mauser M1871 single-shot and M1871/84 magazine rifles, subsequently with the 7.92mm smokeless-powder Mauser/Mannlicher M1888, and finally with the Mauser M1898. Few post garrisons had support weapons heavier than a couple of Maxim machine guns, though each African colony had a few light artillery pieces. If necessary, a Schutztruppe could be reinforced by landing parties from German warships, German marines from the Sea Battalions, or Army expeditionary units temporarily formed in Germany.

Note that the uniforms of the Schutztruppen and Polizeitruppen are described in the Plate Commentaries and photo captions.

AFRICAN COLONIES

TOGOLAND (from 1905, Togo)

Roughly equivalent to modern Togo, this narrow strip ran some 340 miles north from the Bight of Benin on the West African coast, and was about 140 miles broad at its widest. It lay between the British Gold Coast (modern Ghana) to the west and French Dahomey (modern Benin) to the east. German missionaries were established among the southern Ewe tribe before 1850, and traders soon set up a coastal station at Anecho.

The most active German explorer in West Africa was Dr Gustav Nachtigal, who, on July 5, 1884 – backed up by the Imperial Navy gunboat SMS *Möwe* – concluded a treaty establishing a protectorate (Schutzgebiet) over some coastal tribes. (Between 1884 and 1891, Togoland was officially one of two separated parts of a single entity, Deutsch-Westafrika, which also included Cameroon.) The protectorate was internationally recognized in 1885–86, its borders subsequently being adjusted in 1897, 1899, and 1904. A port was established at Lomé, infrastructure and agriculture were developed efficiently, and Togoland would become Germany's only colony actually to produce a profit. A radio station installed at Kamina was also crucially important to wider German operations.

The Ewe population south of the central hills was fragmented into small clans, so easy to dominate in detail. As plantations and road- and rail-building increased, so the exactions of forced labor became increasingly harsh and resented, but there was little resistance in the south. In the mid-1890s, however, expeditions into the northwestern savannah country came into contact with more cohesive tribes, the Dagomba and Konkomba.

The battle of Adibo, 1896

On November 30, 1896 news reached the Dagomba capital, Yendi, of the destruction of a village to the south by a German column. King Andani II ordered the clan chiefs to assemble their forces, but the German advance was too swift for many of them to arrive in time. The column was 368 strong; it was led by Dr Gruner, with 1st Lt von Massow commanding Lt Thierry, Sgt Heitmann, and 91 native rankers of the Togo Polizeitruppe. Of the 277 porters, 46 also had rifles. (The Ghanaian account does not mention machine guns; since it stresses the Africans' shock at encountering breech-loading rifles, we can assume that any Maxim guns would certainly have been mentioned.) The confrontation took place on December 4 in front of the village of Adibo, some 9 miles south of Yendi.

The war chief Kanbonna-kpema Wohu ("Great Warrior Snake") drew up his men at the top of a slope in a line about 1,000 yards long. Ghanaian sources number them at about 4,630, of whom some 2,500 had flintlock muskets, 2,000 were archers, and 130 were horsemen with spears. They were drawn up in three divisions, screened in front b Konkomba archers, and backed by the horsemen held back to exploit any enemy retreat. Von Massow's police, apparently armed with single-shot, bolt-action 1871 Mausers, were drawn up in three platoons; they were followed by the porters, with Dr Gruner bringing up the rear with the rifle-armed porters ready to deploy right or left. Their approach through scrub and tall crops had at one point forced them into single file, but the Dagomba failed to take advantage of this. Von Massow halted about 300 yards from the African line, and ordered volley-fire to provoke the Dagomba into a charge.

Kanbonna-kpema urged his men forward to envelop the small German force on both flanks, but long before they could close to the short range of their old muskets they came under a withering rapid fire. This first encounter with breech-loading weapons was traumatic, but the war chief ordered his warriors to break up into small groups and infiltrate forward. Some got to within about 30 yards, but they were still unable to close to hand-to-hand; eventually they were forced to fall back, and von Massow's men drove them up the slope. The Dagomba left perhaps 430 dead on the field, including their war chief; German casualties were supposedly about 25 percent, including Sgt Heitmann killed. The Dagomba fled their villages and took refuge in the bush, and when the column reached Yendi it was a ghost town. They looted and burned the capital before withdrawing. Resistance continued intermittently for some three years thereafter, but finally collapsed amid internecine conflict.

* * *

A paramilitary Polizeitruppe was formed in 1885 at Lomé, and gradually expanded. This was very similar to a Schutztruppe; the native ranks wore khaki uniform, and were armed with Mauser rifles and, in time, a few

White summer tropical uniforms were used in nearly all of the German colonies, and by all ranks. This group photo taken in Cameroon shows officers and other ranks wearing a variety of white uniforms, with standing or stand-and-fall collars, with or without breast pockets, and with or without colored piping. (AdeQ HA)

machine guns. In 1914 the German cadre consisted of one commandant, one lieutenant, six police superintendent NCOs, one medical NCO, and one artificer, with about 560 native Polizei-Soldaten. Spread between nine districts, the companies might number 60–120 men – for example, 144 were stationed at Lomé, and 109 men were reported to be at Sogode in 1909. Platoons were organized on the basis of tribal background (initially many came from Nigeria).

On the outbreak of World War I an additional 600-odd Africans were recalled to service or recruited anew. These were administratively formed into a battalion, with headquarters at Lomé and detachments at various outstations, including a small mounted contingent in the Sansane Mangu district. The same British reports also mention 550 Mausers in store for arming Africans, and a supply of soft-nosed ammunition. The German population also provided some 200 reservists, who formed a Europäer-Kompagnie to defend Kamina (note that this pre-1929 spelling for "company" is correct).

CAMEROON (1891–96: German West Africa, including Togoland; 1896–1901: German Northwest Africa)

Cameroon (Kamerun) had an area of perhaps 184,000 square miles, stretching northeast and east from a 220-mile north-south coastline on the Gulf of Biafra. British Nigeria lay to the north; the small Atlantic enclave of Spanish Guinea immediately to the southwest; and the huge expanse of French Equatorial Africa ("Middle Congo") to the south and east, with Cameroon's northeastern tip stretching right up to Lake Chad. Today this territory lies mainly in the Republic of Cameroon, with parts in Nigeria, the Central African Republic, Chad, and Gabon.

The Woermann company, and later that of Jantzen & Thormählen, had been active on the coast since 1868, and on July 15, 1884 Gustav Nachtigal concluded a treaty of protection with coastal chiefs (thus forestalling by a matter of days attempts to do the same by both Britain and France). The capital was the port of Duala until 1910, when it moved inland to Buea. The protectorate was internationally recognized in

Cameroon Schutztruppe *askaris* **presenting arms to their commanding officer; the uniforms are those worn from their formation until 1916 – see Plate F4. The German officers and senior NCOs are wearing white tropical uniforms and cork helmets. (AdeQ HA)**

1884–85, and became a colony in 1891. Border agreements with Britain and France were reached in 1897 and 1906, and a further expansion of 107,000 square miles to the south and east was agreed with France in 1911. (As was normal in such cases, the lines on the map enclosed huge areas that were still unexplored.)

In fall 1884 the Yoss tribe rebelled against the imposition of the protectorate, but was quickly suppressed after the arrival in December of the SMS *Bismarck* and *Olga*, which shelled coastal villages and landed bluejackets. Penetration beyond the coastal strip was slow due to the mountainous, forested terrain, but coastal chiefs resented the threat to their monopoly of trade with the interior. The native Polizeitruppe Kamerun was founded in 1889 under Capt Baron Karl von Gravenreuth, with recruits mainly from outside the territory. It saw action in 1891 – alongside sailors from SMS *Habicht* and *Hyäne* – against an Abo tribal rising.

In 1893 Freiherr von Gravenreuth expanded his police force by the ancient African method of buying slaves – 370 of them, from the King of Dahomey; the idea was that they would earn their freedom by five years' service. However, the captain was killed in a skirmish with Buea warriors later that year, and the subsequent cruel treatment of the Dahomeyans' families sparked a mutiny by about 50 of these slave-police in December 1893. After killing their commanders and burning government buildings they were eventually suppressed, once again by sailors mainly from SMS *Hyäne*. A composite marine company drawn from the 1st and 2nd Sea Battalions arrived too late to see action.

The Imperial government established a Schutztruppe on June 9, 1895; its strength was originally 10, later 12 companies each of 150 men. Initial recruiting among Sudanese veterans of the Anglo-Egyptian army failed due to their inability to endure the climate, but later askaris were successfully enlisted from the Yaounda, Bule, Bali, Haussa, and other tribes. Schutztruppe companies saw action on many occasions during the penetration of the interior, which was stubbornly resisted – for example, the station at Yaoundé was often cut off by hostiles – but only in an uncoordinated way. By the early 1900s the colony was pacified; the recall of the brutal governor Jesko von Puttkammer in 1906 improved the situation, though severe exactions of plantation labor continued.

* * *

By 1914 the peacetime strength of the Schutztruppe Kamerun was about 185 German officers, NCOs, and specialists, with 1,650 askaris; they were divided between 49 garrisons, with the headquarters at Soppo near the capital,

This African musician, captioned as belonging to a Kamerun Kompagnie, wears basically the same 1896 corduroy *Waffenrock* as his German counterparts in Southwest Africa, though the red colony-colored cuffs lack *Litzen* or buttons. The "swallow's-nest" shoulder wings are in khaki and red. His *Südwester* hat displays the Imperial cockade and red brim-edging. (AdeQ HA)

Buea. Nine of the 12 field companies were organized into three main groups by regions:

Northwestern Region: 2.FK (Bamenda, Wum, & Kentu); 6.FK (general reserve – Soppo, Mbaiki, Nola, & Nguku); 8.FK (Djang/Ngaundere)
Southeastern Region: 5.FK (Buar, Carnot, & Ebelowa); 9.FK (Dume, Baturi); 10.FK (Yaoundé, Oje, & Mimwoul)
"Islam" Group: 3.FK (Mora & Kusseri); 4.FK (survey/expeditionary company – Soppo, Banyo); 7.FK (Garua, Marua, & Mubi).

Additionally, the 11. Feldkompagnie was stationed at Akoafim and Minkebe in the south, and the 12th at Bumo, Fianga, and Gore in the north. The 1st (Depot) Company, and an artillery detachment with four 9cm C/73 M91 field guns, were both headquartered at the port of Duala.

By that date the Polizeitruppe, controlled by the civil authorities, had increased from about 675 personnel to some 28 Europeans and 1,255 Africans. Many of them had previously served with the Schutztruppe, and were considered professional enough to provide a military reserve in emergencies. The police were mainly dispersed in the south and southwest of the protectorate, at Ossidinge, Victoria, Duala, Edea, Yaoundé, Kribi, and various minor posts. Several former military stations in the south – e.g. Kribi, Victoria, and Buea – now had only a police presence, the troops having moved further north.

On the outbreak of the Great War the Polizeitruppe companies were incorporated into the Schutztruppe. Together with recalled reservists and civilian volunteers, this brought the total German strength in the colony to 34 companies, with 1,460 Germans and 6,550 Africans, but they were handicapped by shortages of weapons and ammunition.

GERMAN SOUTHWEST AFRICA

This region, stretching inland from the South Atlantic coast, covered roughly 322,500 square miles of what is today Namibia, lying between Angola to the north, Botswana to the east, and South Africa to the south. A treaty with Britain in 1890 added the narrow, 280-mile Caprivi Strip thrusting eastward from the northeast corner of the colony to reach the Zambezi River. German Southwest Africa was to be the arena for the most serious fighting, and the most brutal reprisals, in Germany's whole overseas empire.

German missionaries arrived in the 1840s, and traders followed. In November 1882 Adolf Lüderitz successfully requested government protection for a new trading station, and bought large tracts of territory from African chiefs. The protectorate was proclaimed in August 1884, and in 1885 a trading conglomerate, the Deutsche Kolonialgesellschaft für Südwest-Afrika (DKGSWA), was granted a monopoly to exploit mineral deposits, which would prove extremely rich. Despite the arid climate and partly desert terrain there was also enough grazing-land to attract some German settlers.

In May 1886 the first Reichs-Kommissar arrived: Dr Heinrich Ernst Göring, father of the more famous Hermann. The first administrative capital was Otjimbingwe (shifted to Windhoek in 1891). The first troops were installed at Otjimbingwe in May 1888: the Truppe des Reichs-Kommissars, with Lt Ulrich von Quitzow, one other officer, five NCOs, and 20 African soldiers recruited from the Nama

Leutnant of the Southwest Africa Schutztruppe in parade dress, c.1894–95. From 1894 the simple light brown corduroy uniforms worn by the original Truppe des Reichs-Kommissars were modified with the addition of cornflower-blue collars and cuffs, the latter in the pointed 'Polish' style of the German Uhlans, and both were adorned with silver *Litzen*. Silver left-shoulder aiguillettes were commonly worn by officers and senior NCOs on parade. This officer wears the *Käppi* originally issued to all ranks of the Schutztruppe (with silver rings denoting officer ranks), before being gradually replaced with the German-style visored field cap from 1896 onward. The gray képi has a blue band and piping, and a small Imperial cockade on the front – see Plate A1. (AdeQ HA)

and Baster ("bastard," i.e. mixed-blood) groups.[1]

The major tribal groups were all semi-nomadic cattle-raisers: the Nama ("Hottentot") in the south, perhaps 20,000 strong; up to 80,000 Herero in the central and northern regions; and about 90,000 Ovambo in the far north (who remained essentially unconquered). The Nama and Herero were not primitive savages; the missionaries had made some converts, traders had introduced European clothing, and from the South African Boers they had acquired some rifles and – significantly, since they used horses – a knowledge of guerrilla tactics.

The variations of uniform seen in this group of mounted Southwest Africa Schutztruppen, including lancers, suggest a transitional date around 1896, when the *Käppi* and cork helmet were being replaced with the slouch hat and the visored field cap. (AdeQ HA)

First Nama Rebellion, 1893–94

In 1890 the near-bankruptcy of the DKGSWA led to the declaration of a crown colony, which soon began to expand inland to secure territory for German settler-farmers. Colonial officials played off one clan against another, signing local treaties to extend their control. However, attempts to force the Witbooi Nama to sign away their lands led to the first real African opposition, led by a chief named Hendrik Witbooi. German officials called upon the Imperial Commissioner's Troop, now commanded by Capt Curt von Francois, to force Hendrik's people to submit; but despite its expansion von Francois still had only a modest force, and needed support from Germany. This came first in the form of the captain's brother, Lt Hugo von Francois, with another officer and 214 German rankers, who arrived at Walvis Bay on March 16, 1893.

(It must be stressed that, in contrast to the other colonial garrisons, the future Kaiserliche Schutztruppe für Deutsch-Südwestafrika – a title not adopted until 1895 – would consist entirely of German volunteers from amongst serving or former Imperial Army and Navy personnel. Organized in the colony as mounted infantry, their strength would reach some 700 men by 1897.)

Captain von Francois set out from Windhoek for Hendrik's stronghold at Hornkranz on April 8, 1893; he had 195 all ranks, in two companies led by his brother and Lt Schwabe. Arriving before the fortified village on April 12, the captain sent his separated companies into the attack from the east and north. Although this achieved surprise, the resistance of the 250-odd warriors (perhaps 100 of them armed with rifles, and 120 with horses) was spirited. However, after three hours' fighting the Witboois were forced to abandon their village, leaving behind some 150 dead including many women and children.

---

[1] Also known as Rehoboth Basters, these were among numerous descendants of Cape Colony Dutchmen, Indian and Malay immigrants, and indigenous Africans – the people known in the apartheid years as "Cape Coloreds." Following the German annexation of Southwest Africa the Basters worked with the colonizers, and served on the German side during the Herero campaigns; consequently they were able to keep their land and cattle, while the Nama and the Herero were dispossessed and driven into concentration camps. This cooperation ended on May 8, 1915, when Germany declared war on the Basters following their refusal to assist the war effort.

This success was short-lived; a Witbooi attack drove off or captured most of the Germans' horses, leaving the troops for a time unable to pursue the well-mounted rebels. Although a further 100 German reinforcements arrived in June 1893, in August a Witbooi ambush completely destroyed a supply train of 20 wagons. That month – after receiving yet another reinforcement of 2 officers, 10 NCOs, and 105 men – the newly promoted Maj von Francois attempted to surround the rebels and force them into a fatal confrontation. However, the mobile Witboois kept slipping away from skirmishes and raiding into the German rear areas. Six months after being forced out of his base Hendrik was stronger than ever, with about 600 men, 400 rifles, and 300 horses. The only time von Francois came close to trapping him was on February 1–2, 1894 in the Onab Valley, but despite fierce fighting including the use of light artillery the Witboois once again managed to slip away into the hills.

That same month, Berlin replaced the discredited commander with Maj Theodor Leutwein. The new governor did not immediately move against the Witbooi Nama, but invested time in negotiating with and winning over neighboring tribes. He thus began to regain control over the southern region while cutting off much of the support that Hendrik had formerly received. In May, Leutwein got Hendrik to agree to a truce until the end of July, which bought time for the arrival of another 250 German reinforcements.

After Hendrik and his followers retreated to fortified positions in the Naukluft Mountains, Leutwein followed him, blocking the passes to prevent any escape. The subsequent battle began on August 27, 1894, and developed into a wide-ranging series of clashes over rough terrain, with both sides contesting control of waterholes and strategic high ground. Losing the last of his waterholes and unable to retreat, Hendrik surrendered on September 9. Under the terms of the treaty the Witboois became allies of the Germans, and would provide them with auxiliaries on a number of later occasions.

Leutwein proceeded to suppress, disarm and sometimes dispossess other groups, in the latter case interning them in camps around Windhoek. For example, in February 1896 he led 100 men into the lands of the Mbandjeru and Khaua Nama. He forced a treaty on the Khaua chief Andreas Lambert, who was required to return cattle raided from another tribe, hand over weapons, and accept German authority. When he broke the terms and tried to escape with his whole tribe, Lambert was arrested and executed; his people were stripped of their weapons and 12,000 cattle, and were interned in labor camps. Other groups who were disarmed between 1896 and 1903, and punished for defiance by at least partial internment, were the so-called "Afrikaners" tribe, the Zwartboois, the Groetfontein mixed-bloods, and the Bondelswarts.

Herero Rebellion, 1904–07

Some Herero tribesmen, traditionally hostile to the Nama, had served the Germans as auxiliaries; but it was this tribal group who would stage the most serious uprising, and who

would suffer the cruelest reprisals. A number of contributory factors included an epidemic in 1897 that killed half of their cattle, and the fact that German settlement was putting mounting pressure on various clans. (By 1902 the colony's white settlers numbered about 2,600 Germans, 1,350 Afrikaner Boers, and 450 British.) Following the 1897 epidemic, large numbers of these proud pastoralists had been reduced to farm labor for German settlers, who treated them abusively. When word spread that the Herero were to be disarmed, on January 12, 1904 the chief Samuel Maherero led a revolt at Okahandja. This took Maj Leutwein completely by surprise; he and three-quarters of his men were at that moment more than 400 miles to the south, suppressing a small rising by the Bondelswart tribe.

Leutwein's active forces then consisted of 40 officers and 726 rankers, divided between four companies of mounted infantry and one of artillery. He also had a potential reserve of 34 officers and 730 former enlisted men; 400 German settlers with no military training; and 250 African scouts and auxiliaries. His troops were armed with the M1888 magazine rifle, and he also had 5 quick-firers, 5 older artillery pieces, and 5 Maxim guns. There were a number of small walled forts scattered around the colony, each with an armory, barracks, and watchtower.

Maherero had 7,000–8,000 warriors, perhaps half of them with firearms (though with little ammunition); in the north they faced only weak opposition, and their rising spread rapidly. Isolated farms and ranches were destroyed, and the Hereros killed at least 120 settlers (though they spared women and children, missionaries, and non-Germans). Most of the settlements and forts in the region were attacked, and both Okahandja and Windhoek were briefly placed under siege. Between January 19 and February 4 troops arrived to relieve both towns, but were not strong enough to take the offensive.

The first reinforcements to arrive, on January 18, were sailors from the cruiser SMS *Habicht*; they would serve ashore throughout the rebellion, and would be joined by Navy gunners and medics. In Germany, two companies each from 1st and 2nd Sea Bns formed a Marine Expeditionary Corps under Maj Glassenap; the survivors would return home in March 1905. A massive reinforcement for the Southwest Africa Schutztruppe was urgently organized, and during February and March 1904 alone 1,576 troops, 1,000 horses, 10 artillery pieces, and 6 machine guns arrived in the colony.

Reinforced to the point where he could put 2,500 men into field, Maj Leutwein launched a three-column counteroffensive in April 1904, but the newly arrived German troops, unaccustomed to the harsh climate, soon proved ineffectual. The 530-strong Eastern Column (including half of Maj Glassenap's marine battalion) was deployed as a stop-line, but in mid-March it took 70 casualties in two indecisive actions, and it retreated in May. The combined Western and Main columns inflicted heavy losses on some 3,000 warriors at Onganjirn, and again while breaking out of an encirclement at Ovimbo, but Leutwein then called off the operation while he awaited further reinforcements.

Leutwein was replaced in June with Gen Lothar von Trotha, a ruthless officer with experience in the HeHe Rebellion (see "German East Africa") and China, who by the end of that month had been reinforced to a strength enabling him to put into the field 10,000 troops with 32 artillery

One contingent of the Southwest Africa Schutztruppe rode on camels, which were judged superior to horses for mounted infantry operating in desert conditions. Trained and organized by Capt Friedrich von Erckert in 1907, they were deployed in the pursuit and capture of the Nama leader Simon Kopper in 1908, among other operations. The animals originally came from the Canary Islands and the Sudan. (AdeQ HA)

pieces. (Total German reinforcements to the colony would reach some 15,000 men.) These resources enabled him to encircle about 6,000 Herero fighters with 4,000 dependents who had dug themselves into positions in the Waterberg Mountains. On August 11 the German force advanced on the Herero stronghold from three directions, leaving the defenders only one possible escape route – onto the waterless Omaheke plain, an arm of the Kalahari Desert. A punishing bombardment was followed by converging infantry assaults.

After the surviving Herero finally broke out into the desert, von Trotha constructed a 150-mile line of guard posts, poisoned the waterholes, put bounties on the heads of Herero leaders, and ordered the shooting on sight of any man who approached the line. His documented orders make quite clear that his aim was expulsion or extermination. He maintained his punitive campaign until recalled in November 1905, after reports of his methods caused an outcry among liberal circles in Germany (though this did not prevent his promotion). Samuel Maherero and a handful of followers managed to escape to claim asylum in British territory, but African deaths from thirst, starvation, outright massacres, and subsequently from cruel and widely documented abuse in concentration and labor camps reached such an appalling level that they have officially been classified (and admitted) as genocide. The Herero population was reduced from an estimated 80,000 before the rebellion to just 15,000 counted in the 1911 census.

Second Nama Rebellion, 1904–08

Bitter enemies of the Herero, the Nama had initially honored the terms of their 1894 treaty. However, when warnings reached him that von Trotha intended to disarm his people too, in October 1904 the 80-year-old Hendrik Witbooi led a second uprising in the south. Although only about one-third of his 1,000–1,500 followers had rifles, and they were outnumbered perhaps 17 to 1, they conducted a long and stubborn guerrilla campaign, fighting more than 200 skirmishes before they were crushed. During the course of the revolt Hendrik was killed near Tses, and leadership passed to Jacob Morenga. In April 1905, Gen von Trotha sent the Nama people an explicit threat that he would subject them to the same fate as the Herero, and he and his successors were as good as his word. It is estimated that up to 10,000 Nama (50 percent of the total population) died during the 1904–08 revolt and its aftermath, and the rest were driven into internment camps or handed over, essentially as slaves, to government and commercial interests needing laborers. Combined German deaths during both these risings are estimated at 1,749.

Troopers of the Bastardsoldaten Kompagnie in about 1905. These mixed-blood soldiers were dressed exactly as their German counterparts, here in very pale examples of the 1896 Schutztruppe *Kord Waffenrock*; under magnification the blue collar and cuffs complete with white *Litzen* are evident. The corduroy field caps, of a darker shade, have a blue band with a small Imperial cockade. Such troops normally wore standard Schutztruppe mounted equipment in brown leather.

LEFT **A new home-service uniform in light stone-gray for all Schutztruppe, authorized on March 11, 1897, had facings and piping in colony colors. To the existing red, blue, and white for Cameroon, Southwest Africa, and East Africa were added, in 1912, yellow for Togo, green for New Guinea, and pink for Samoa. The enlisted ranks' shoulder straps in Imperial colors for all colonies remained unchanged. See under Plate D1 for further details. (AdeQ HA)**

RIGHT **The first Landespolizei, raised in 1905, wore Schutztruppe uniforms with red trim and police insignia, but on September 28, 1907 a new uniform was authorized. In dark khaki-brown with a green collar and shoulder straps, this bore rank insignia in the form of sunburst "pips" on the collar, and green cuff-rings – here, the single pip and looped cuff-ring of a Polizeisergeant. See under Plate G2 for further details. (AdeQ HA)**

Schutztruppe, 1908–14

Most of the many thousands of reinforcements returned home, and the Schutztruppe in the colony resumed a peacetime footing. Its strength by 1914 was 91 officers, 342 NCOs, 1,444 enlisted men, plus about 100 doctors, technical specialists, and administrators, for a total of 1,967 personnel. The great majority were Germans, but there were also some Austrians and some Afrikaner Boers in the ranks. The headquarters were at Windhoek, and the field companies and artillery batteries were organized under two district commands:

Northern District (HQ Windhoek)
1.FK (Regenstein, Seeis); 4.FK (Okanjande); 6.FK (Outjo, Otavi); 2. Batterie (Johann-Albrechts-Höhe)

Southern District (HQ Keetmanshoop)
2.FK (Ukamas); 3.FK (Kanus); 5.FK (Chamis, Churutabis); 7. & 8.FK (camel-mounted – Gochas, Arahoab); 1. Batterie (Narubis); 3. Batterie (Gibeon).

There was also a twelfth field unit, termed the Bastardsoldaten Kompagnie, which was recruited from nonlocal Africans and men of mixed blood.

Territorial Police

The Kaiserliche Landespolizei für Deutsch Südwestafrika was first raised on March 1, 1905. During 1907 it reached an establishment of 400 men, and also took delivery of its first motor vehicle, though the horse and camel remained the standard means of transport. This force carried small arms but performed police rather than paramilitary duties. In 1914 its peacetime strength was 7 German officers and 500 German enlisted men, with 50 African auxiliaries.

GERMAN EAST AFRICA

This territory stretched for some 384,000 square miles inland from the Indian Ocean, comprising roughly modern Tanzania, Rwanda, and Burundi. It was bounded to the north by British East Africa (modern Kenya and Uganda); to the west by the Belgian Congo; to the southwest and south by British Northern Rhodesia and Nyasaland (modern Zambia and Malawi); and to the southeast by Portuguese East Africa (modern Mozambique).

The coast had been settled by Arabs since medieval times, and their traders and slavers had later penetrated the interior. The most important tribal groupings were – roughly from north to south – part of the Masai, the Ngoni, and the HeHe, each with their subject peoples. Additionally, a freebooting warrior caste known as the Ruga-Ruga were still significant. Tribal wars in East

Africa were frequent and fiercely fought; the colonizers would exploit these enmities, hiring client chiefs to do much of their work, and Ruga-Ruga as auxiliaries.

In 1884, Karl Peters of the German East African Company (Deutsch-Ostafrikanische Gesellschaft, DOAG) concluded treaties with various inland chiefs. In February 1885 he obtained an Imperial charter, and in 1886 France and Britain recognized German interests in the interior. The ruler of the offshore Arab island Sultanate of Zanzibar was forced to renounce his claims on the mainland under the guns of German warships. In 1888, coastal Arab leaders resisted the attempted expansion of the company's holdings; the DOAG requested government help, and on January 1, 1891 an Imperial protectorate was declared. (A separate, unsuccessful venture by the brothers Denhardt, whose Tana Company obtained a small enclave in Wituland near the northern port of Lamu in April 1885, had been absorbed by the DOAG in 1888; under a treaty with Britain in June–July 1890 the Imperial authorities ceded all of Wituland to British East Africa.)

Abushiri (Arab) Rebellion, 1888–90

Sparked by resentment over the DOAG's commercial and territorial ambitions, this rising was instigated by the wealthy Abushiri ibn Salim al-Harthi, whose 8,000 followers included both fellow Arabs and coastal African tribesmen. From September 20, 1888 they attacked or besieged German trading posts and towns in the north, including the then capital, Bagamoyo. After fierce fighting a German naval landing party 260 strong saved Bagamoyo, and a rebel attack on Dar es Salaam (which would become the capital in 1890) was also repulsed. A former Imperial Army officer who was available in-country, Hermann von Wissmann, was appointed Reichs-Kommissar and authorized to raise a unit in 1889. He received 22 German officers and 40 NCOs, and enlisted about 1,000 Africans into seven companies – some 600 veteran Sudanese askaris, and 400 mercenaries including Somalis and local Ngoni warriors. This Wissmanntruppe had shortened M1871 Jäger rifles, but only one machine gun.

At the head of this force and with coastal help from the Navy, the new commissioner systematically crushed the rebellion, and the hostile forces began to fragment. On May 8, 1889 he stormed Abushiri's stronghold of Jahazi, but the rebel leader escaped inland and continued his resistance aided by Yao and Mbunga tribesmen. In December, however, the Germans' continued successes prompted the Africans to turn Abushiri in, and his hanging marked the end of the revolt.

Wissmann's askaris provided the nucleus for the new Kaiserliche Schutztruppe für Deutsch-Ostafrika, authorized by the Reichstag on March 22, 1891. The officers and NCOs were the usual German volunteers with previous military experience. The askaris, organized in field companies about 150 strong, continued to be a mixture of Sudanese and local recruits, the latter being posted to towns and small forts away from their home regions. In time this distinction would fade, and the whole force gained a reputation for loyalty, discipline, and high morale.

HeHe Rebellion, 1891–98

The HeHe (Wahehe) of the south-central region were an aggressive federation welded together by the father of their present chief Mkwawa.

This group photo shows the three types of uniforms authorized on June 4, 1891 for the German officers and NCOs of the new East African Schutztruppe. The dark blue uniform was piped in white; the white tropical uniform was piped in blue, and a khaki cotton field uniform in yellow. Note that all three types have "Brandenburg" cuff-flaps. (The yellow piping would be discontinued after the introduction in 1896 of the new khaki uniform piped in blue for all colonies.) Each tunic bore yellow-metal Imperial crown badges on the collar, and NCOs wore chevrons on the left sleeve. Previously, the German personnel of the original Truppe des Reichs-Kommissars von Wissmann in 1889–91 had worn white tropical helmets with the Imperial cockade, a white service uniform, and a dark blue tunic for full dress. The latter had a stand-and-fall collar, brass buttons, and silver shoulder cords with red and black threads; officers had one to three gold rank rings round the cuffs, the top one looped, and wore sashes and sword knots in silver, red, and black. On a khaki service dress of the same pattern, NCOs displayed one to three rank chevrons on the left upper sleeve. The askaris wore a red fez with a blue tassel or a wraparound turban, single-breasted khaki tunics, and blue puttees. Most leather equipment used in the German colonies was of brown leather. (AdeQ HA)

In July 1891, border frictions prompted Commissioner Emil von Zelewski to lead a three-company punitive column toward the HeHe stronghold at Iringa, burning villages as he went. On August 27 – with his 13 German officers and NCOs, 320 askaris, and 170 porters strung out in rocky terrain – he was ambushed by 3,000 warriors led by Mkwawa's brother Mpangie. Although mostly armed with spears, the HeHe inflicted the worst massacre ever suffered by German colonial troops, killing the commissioner and 361 of his men (9 other Germans, 256 askaris, and 96 porters).

Tit-for-tat attacks continued for three years while the new commissioner, Col Baron von Schelle, prepared the ground by forging alliances with other tribes. In October 1894 he led a cautious new advance with 609 askaris and three Maxim guns. Although protected by a moat and a 12-foot wall, Iringa was taken on October 30; Mkwanga escaped, and guerrilla warfare continued until July 1898 when, finally cornered, the chief killed himself.

Maji-Maji Rebellion, 1905–07

Taxed heavily and reduced to agricultural servitude, southeastern tribes led by the Kibata rebelled in July 1905. A witch doctor had preached that a magic potion, Maji-Maji, could stop German bullets, and several other tribes quickly joined the rising. With only 588 Schutztruppe askaris and 458 police in the south the Germans were unable to contain the outbreak; missions and trading posts were destroyed, Mahenge and Songea were besieged, and soon about 20 percent of the colony was in rebel hands.

On August 30, some 4,000 Mbunga and Pogoro tribesmen attacked Mahenge; having few guns, they relied mostly upon spears, poisoned arrows, and the protection of their magic. The 60-strong garrison under

Lt von Hassel had a Maxim gun, and repulsed the human-wave attacks with heavy loss, though they would remain besieged for two more months. Another important defeat took place on October 21 at Namabengo, where some 5,000 Ngoni warriors gathering to attack the garrison were scattered by Capt Nigmann's audacious preemptive night attack with just 117 askaris. Such setbacks broke the rebels' confidence in Maji-Maji; the rebellion faltered, and failed to spread to more northern tribes such as the HeHe, who had already learned a painful lesson.

The outbreak had caused alarm in Berlin, which responded to Governor von Götzen's appeals by sending two cruisers, and a two-company Marine Expeditionskorps under Capt von Schlichting drawn from the Seebataillone; in all, 1,000 men from Germany landed in October 1905. The marine companies were split up among the Schutztruppe and used mainly in a defensive role, until repatriated early in 1907.

(Count von Götzen also appealed directly to Governor Hahl in German New Guinea, and in January 1906 about 150 Buka tribal Polizei-Soldaten from Bougainville in the Solomons were shipped all the way to East Africa. However, during their training on arrival under the command of Lt Phillip Correck they were deemed unfit for service, due both to their small physique and susceptibility to local diseases. They were employed only on garrison duties, and were shipped home after a few months.)

In October 1905 Count von Götzen sent three columns into rebel country, killing and laying waste as they advanced. Despite a successful ambush by Bena warriors at the Ruhuji River crossing the southwest had been pacified by April 1906, and the rising in the southeast degenerated into intermittent guerrilla fighting. Amid a devastating famine, this guttered out in August 1907. It is estimated that the rebellion cost several hundred German lives, but up to 75,000 among the African population.

* * *

Askaris in all the German African colonies wore a khaki uniform based on that of the original Sudanese recruits from the Anglo-Egyptian army – see Plates D3 & G1. These askaris from German East Africa are identified by their distinctive *tarbush* headgear. Originally worn without insignia, though occasionally with metal company numerals, it received a white-metal Imperial eagle badge in 1896 (see Plate H2); a larger brass version was worn by the Polizeitruppe. (AdeQ HA)

By 1914 the peacetime strength of the East Africa Schutztruppe was 68 German officers, 60 German and 184 African NCOs, and 2,286 rankers, plus 132 German medical officers, technical specialists, and administrators. They were organized in 14 field companies of 160 (expandable to 200), each *Feldkompagnie* with an additional 250 porters and some attached "Ruga-Ruga" irregulars acting as scouts. Headquarters and central services were at Dar es Salaam, and the companies were dispersed as follows:

1.FK (Arusha/Neu Moshi); 2.FK (Iringa, Ubena); 3.FK (Lindi); 4.FK (Dodoma); 5.FK (Massocko/Langenburg); 6.FK (Udjidji, Kassulo); 7.FK (Bukoba, Ussuwi, Kifumbiro); 8.FK (Tabora); 9.FK (Urundi); 10.FK (Dar es Salaam); 11.FK (Kissenji, Mruhengeri – Rwanda); 12.FK (Mahenge); 13.FK (Koanda-Iringi); and 14.FK (Mwanza, Ikoma).

Only the 1st, 4th, 8th, 10th, and 13th Cos had yet received the latest *Gewehr 98* rifle, the rest carrying the old 11mm M1871/84 Jäger magazine rifle taking black-powder cartridges. Each company had two 7.92mm Maxim MGs, and one or two 3.7cm light artillery pieces; the latter could be concentrated into a single Artillerie-Abteilung. (Guns had to be small enough to be broken down for man-carrying where necessary; in East Africa the endemic "sleeping sickness" spread by the tsetse fly ruled out the use of horses by troops and gun-teams alike.) Each field company had a large cadre of 16–20 German officers and NCOs, and – uniquely in the German colonies – two African *effendi* officers. On April 13, 1914, LtCol Paul von Lettow-Vorbeck assumed command and began a retraining program.

In 1914 the separate Polizeitruppe had roughly 65 German officers, NCOs, and specialist personnel, and 2,000 askaris, many of them veterans of the Schutztruppe. On the outbreak of war these men were reintegrated into the field companies.

PACIFIC POSSESSIONS

German New Guinea and associated island groups

In 1884 the German New Guinea Company raised the Imperial flag over the northeastern part of modern Papua New Guinea (then known as Kaiser-Wilhelmsland), and what is still called the Bismarck Archipelago – modern New Britain and New Ireland (then known respectively as Neu-Pommern, "New Pomerania," and Neu-Mecklenburg). Other Melanesian and Micronesian islands in the Southwest Pacific were soon added to the protectorate: the Marshall and Caroline islands and Palau in 1885; three of the Solomon Islands in 1886 (of which only Bougainville and Buka were retained after 1899); Nauru in 1888, and finally the

Marianas (except for American Guam) in 1899.[2] In that year administration was transferred to the Colonial Office, and a Polizeitruppe was established with a handful of German NCOs. The rankers were recruited from Malays in the Dutch East Indies, some of whom had previous Dutch military service. There were originally 12 policemen in the West Carolines, 22 in the East Carolines, and 12 in the Marianas.

There was only one significant uprising in the Southwest Pacific colonies. In 1910 the Sokehs people on Ponape in the East Carolines rose up under a chief named Soumadau, in resentment (as so often elsewhere) over the German use of forced labor. The rebels killed Carl Boeder, the local German governor, two other Germans, and five islanders working for them. As there was no radio communication with the outside world, it was several weeks before news reached Rabaul. A German police officer, a judge, and some 300 Polizei-Soldaten armed with carbines and machetes were shipped from New Guinea, backed by bluejackets from the SMS *Emden, Comoran,* and *Nürnberg.* The rebels had taken to the bush by the time the Germans occupied their stronghold in an old fort, but were later rounded up; the ringleaders were shot, and the Sokehs population was deported to Palau.

By 1914 the Polizeitruppe in German New Guinea and the Southwest Pacific islands consisted of 27 Germans and 932 natives, dispersed as follows: Kaiser-Wilhelmsland, 670; East Carolines, 122; West Carolines, 71; Marianas, 30; and Marshalls, 39. In addition, 12 were serving as customs and harbor police.

Melanesian Polizei-Soldaten in German New Guinea wore a dark red *sarong* and some form of German headgear as their only signs of uniform, and their appearance was often very irregular. Of interest is the Germans' toleration of traditional adornments such as animal bones and teeth, plant fibers strung with seashells, pieces of coral, beads, etc; these were worn around the neck, upper arms and wrists, in the hair, or even through the nose. (AdeQ HA)

Samoa

There had been German trading stations and coconut plantations in the Central Pacific archipelago of Samoa since the 1850s. The German naval presence increased during the 1880s, and following negotiations with Britain and the USA the islands of Upolu and Savai'i were recognized as a German protectorate in 1899. The people of Samoa were generally peaceful; consequently German rule was less harsh than in the African colonies, and there were only two significant incidents before 1914.

In 1888, before Germany formally took possession, a Samoan chief named Mataafa led an armed rising against German traders and settlers. About 150 sailors from SMS *Olga, Eber,* and *Adler* were landed near Apia to confront the rebels, and in the ensuing battle of Vailele the Germans suffered 16 dead and 39 wounded.

[2] Melanesia includes the Bismarck Archipelago, the Louisade, Solomon, Santa Cruz, New Hebrides, and Loyalty islands, New Caledonia, Fiji, and intervening groups. Micronesia, further north, includes the Mariana, Marshall, Caroline, and Gilbert islands.

In 1908–11 an indigenous resistance movement known as Mau A Pule was causing unease, and about 100 Polizei-Soldaten were shipped from German New Guinea as a precaution. The unrest was quelled without significant violence in 1911, when the Germans arrested and exiled the movement's leader.

The Samoan Polizeitruppe (*Leo-Leo*) was a small, locally recruited force commanded by German police NCOs; in 1914 they numbered 2 European superintendents and 52 Samoans. In addition, there was a ceremonial guard about 30 strong, known as *Fita-Fita* ("soldiers"), recruited only from the sons of tribal chieftains. They were armed with obsolete breech-loading rifles, and had one elderly artillery piece that was fired once a day from Apia harbor.

THE GERMAN PRESENCE IN CHINA

In 1898, China was forced to grant Germany a 99-year lease on Jiaozhou (in German, Kiautschou) and about 200 square miles of territory around Jiaozhou Bay on the southern coast of the Shandong Peninsula. The Germans then developed the port of Qingdao (Tsingtao/Tsingtau) on the eastern headland of the bay as a base for the Navy's East Asian Squadron, which operated in support of German territories in the Pacific. After the Boxer Rebellion (1900–01), the landward and seaward defenses of the town and port were considerably strengthened.

Local recruitment

The III. Seebataillon arrived to garrison the Tsingtao concession in January 1898, and in February 1899 it formed a local Chinesekompagnie with 120 foot and 20 mounted soldiers led by 3 German officers and 10 NCOs. The experiment proved disappointing, with a high level of desertions. In 1900 the company was reduced to 56 infantrymen and

12 troopers for police and garrison duties, and it would finally be absorbed into the native police force in 1909.

Almost concurrently, six Chinese policemen were recruited in 1898 to maintain law and order amongst the growing Chinese population of Tsingtao. Their number increased to 28 Polizei-Soldaten (also known as "gendarmes") in 1899, and to 60 by 1914, some being mounted. This Tsingtau Polizeitruppe was also led by a German cadre from the III. Seebataillon.

East Asian Expeditionary Corps and Occupation Brigade

At the outbreak of the Boxer Rebellion in June 1900 the garrison of the German concessions comprised the III. Seebataillon with 1,126 men, a marine artillery battery, some 800 men of a "Kommando Detachment," and sailors from the East Asian Squadron. To reinforce them, the Ostasiatische Expeditionskorps was created: a force of about 15,000 (mostly) volunteers from the regular Army, organized under the command of Gen Alfred Count von Waldersee. It comprised initially 4, later 6 two-battalion infantry regiments and a Jäger company; single regiments of cavalry and field artillery; single battalions of heavy artillery, engineers, and train; and service units. On landing, it additionally incorporated the Marine-Expeditionskorps (I. & II. Seebataillone) that had preceded it to China by a few weeks.

The first elements of the Corps arrived at Taku on September 21, too late to take part in any of the major actions, but while mainly employed

Bicyclists serving with the East Asian Expeditionary Corps during the Boxer Rebellion – see Plate B1. Note the white shoulder strap with a large stitched red numeral "1", for the 1st (Prussian) Regt of the Corps. (AdeQ HA)

Cork helmets, *Pickelhauben*, and visored field caps can all be seen among this group of soldiers of the East Asian Occupation Brigade. They wear the new uniform introduced, in both light field-gray (*feldgrau*) and khaki, over the turn of 1900/01; this featured a four-pocket *Litewka* tunic with concealed buttons, and red piping for all arms of service – see Plate B3. The tropical helmet had an Imperial eagle plate, and a cloth band in arm-of-service color: white for infantry; red, cavalry (see right-hand standing man, with bandolier and leather-reinforced riding trousers); black with red piping, artillery and engineers; blue, supply train; and dark blue with red piping, medical. (AdeQ HA)

for garrison duties the Germans did fight a number of smaller engagements against remaining pockets of Boxers. When the Corps was largely disbanded and recalled to Germany early in 1901, a smaller force was created on May 17 for continuing occupation duties. This East Asian Occupation Brigade (Ostasiatische Besatzungsbrigade) consisted of 3 infantry regiments and a mounted squadron, 3 field artillery batteries, an engineer and a train company, and service units. The 3rd Inf Regt, 3rd Arty Bty, and some service units were disbanded in May 1902, and 2nd Arty Bty in December 1902. Now with a strength of 1,100 men, the brigade was retitled the East Asian Detachment, and based primarily at the international concessions in Beijing (Peking) and Tianjin (Tientsin).

In April 1909 the Army contingent was finally withdrawn, being replaced by the Navy's East Asian Marine Detachment. Apart from those

(continued on page 33)

GERMAN SOUTHWEST AFRICA, 1890s
1: *Major, c.1894–96*
2: *Reiter,* corduroy uniform, from 1896
3: *Reiter, Kord Waffenrock, c.1897*
4: *Unteroffizier, Kord Litewka, c.1897*

A

CHINA, 1900–14
1: *Soldat*, 1st (Prussian) Regt, E. Asian Expeditionary Corps, 1900–01
2: *Polizei-Soldat*, Chinese *Tsingtau Polizeitruppe*, 1909–14
3: *Kanonier*, 1st E. Asian Fd Arty Bn, E. Asian Occupation Bde, 1901–09

B

SEEBATAILLONE , 1893–1918
1: *Seesoldat, I. Seebataillon*; Kiel, *c.*1900
2: *Sergeant, III. Seebataillon*; Tsingtao, 1914
3: *Seesoldat, 1. Marine Division*; Belgium, 1917–18

C

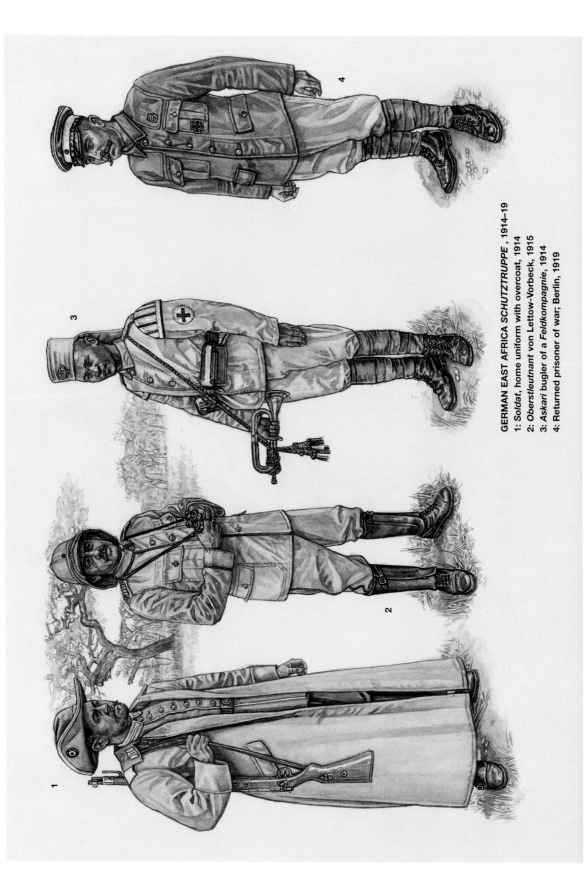

GERMAN EAST AFRICA SCHUTZTRUPPE, 1914–19

1: *Soldat*, home uniform with overcoat, 1914
2: *Oberstleutnant* von Lettow-Vorbeck, 1915
3: *Askari* bugler of a *Feldkompagnie*, 1914
4: Returned prisoner of war; Berlin, 1919

D

COLONIAL AUXILIARY TROOPS, 1914–18
1: Reservist, *Schützenkompagnie*; German E. Africa, 1914–18
2: Reservist, German New Guinea, 1914
3: Volunteer, *Bürgerwehr*; Samoa, 1914
4: Reservist, Cameroon, 1914

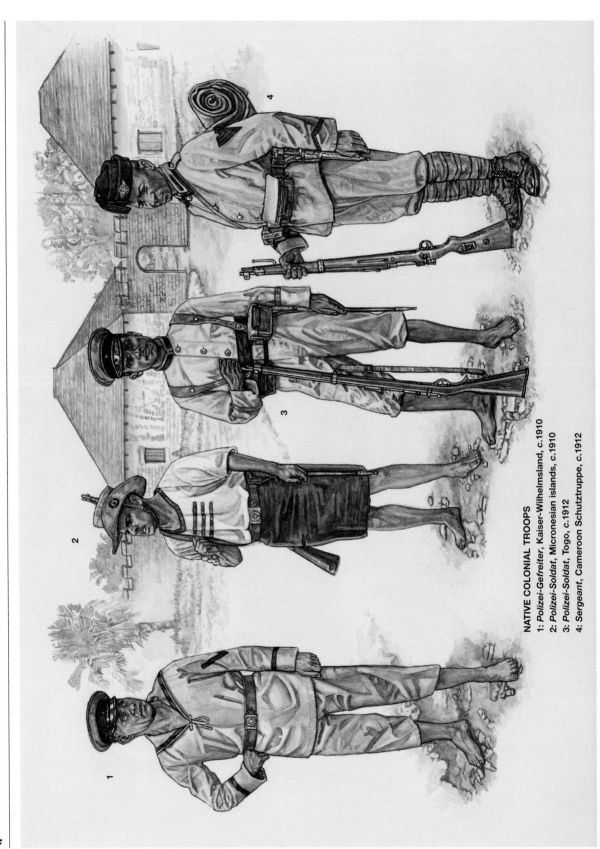

F

NATIVE COLONIAL TROOPS

1: Polizei-Gefreiter, Kaiser-Wilhelmsland, c.1910
2: Polizei-Soldat, Micronesian islands, c.1910
3: Polizei-Soldat, Togo, c.1912
4: Sergeant, Cameroon Schutztruppe, c.1912

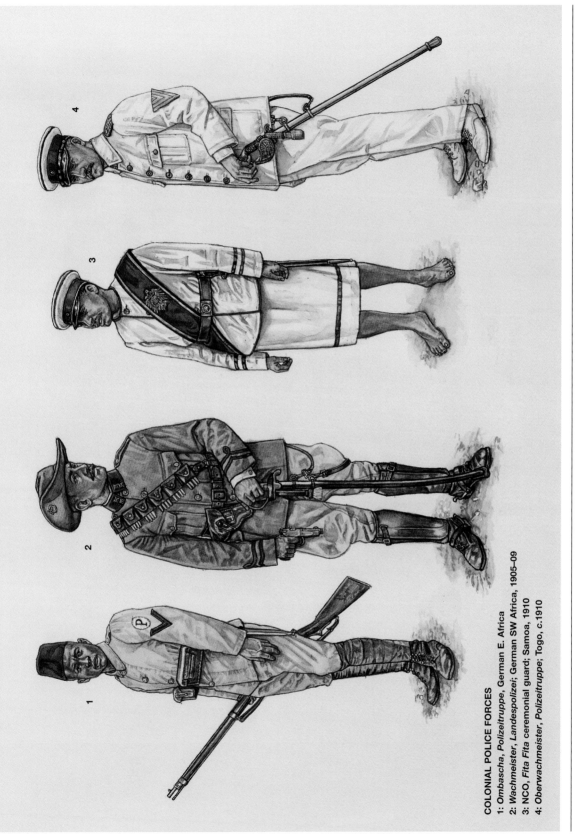

COLONIAL POLICE FORCES

1: *Ombascha, Polizeitruppe, German E. Africa*

2: *Wachmeister, Landespolizei; German SW Africa, 1905–09*

3: *NCO, Fita Fita ceremonial guard; Samoa, 1910*

4: *Oberwachmeister, Polizeitruppe; Togo, c.1910*

G

INSIGNIA & DECORATIONS
See commentary text for details

at Peking and Tientsin, this maintained a garrison of sailors and marines at Kiautschou; with infantry, mounted infantry, artillery, and service units, the Detachment totaled 2,456 officers and men, and an additional 400 reservists could be called out if required. There was also an armed police force with 32 Europeans and about 100 Chinese.

THE SEA BATTALIONS

The first German naval infantry were organized at Stettin on May 13, 1852. This Marinier-Korps provided small contingents for maintaining discipline aboard warships and carrying out limited landing operations. By 1870 the first Seebataillon, with headquarters at Kiel on the Baltic coast, had a strength of 22 officers and 682 NCOs and men. After the establishment of the Reich in 1871, Bismarck's entire focus was on continental politics, and he was so little concerned with the Navy that a Prussian lieutenant-general, Albrecht von Stosch, was appointed to head the new Imperial Admiralty.

Von Stosch ended the practice of detaching parties of marines aboard warships, and ordered the training of formed battalions of naval infantry for landing operations. The original battalion was enlarged to six companies; half were then transferred to Wilhelmshaven on the North Sea coast to form the II. Seebataillon, and each unit was brought up to four companies. Army officers were exchanged into these battalions to introduce current tactical thinking (among others, 1st Lt Erich Ludendorff served as a company commander in 1888–91, and LtCol Paul von Lettow-Vorbeck as commanding officer of the 2nd Sea Bn, 1909–13).

After the occupation of Kiautschou in China on November 14, 1897 by the Navy's East Asian Cruiser Squadron, two companies each from the two battalions were combined to form the III. Seebataillon, which arrived at Tsingtao on January 26, 1898 to garrison the Navy's East Asian Station. It was then, and remained, the only all-German unit with permanent status to be stationed in an overseas protectorate.

As already mentioned, from the mid-1880s onward composite expeditionary units of Sea Battalion troops were periodically deployed overseas as temporary intervention forces to reinforce the Schutztruppen. One company was sent from Germany to Cameroon in 1884. During the Boxer Rebellion, 1st Lt Count von Sodern of the III. Seebataillon led 50 men from Tsingtao to Peking, where they took part in the defense of the Legations. The first reinforcements to arrive from Germany, in August, were I. & II. Seebataillone; thereafter, as the Combined Marine Regiment with artillery and engineer support, they formed a brigade within the East Asian Expeditionary Corps. A composite marine battalion supported the Southwest Africa Schutztruppe during the Herero and Nama

LEFT **This photograph of a marine (Seesoldat) in peacetime service dress shows the black leather Jäger-style shako dressed for parade with an enveloping black horsehair plume; the raised oval cockade in Imperial colors surmounts a brass eagle-and-anchor plate. The 1893 tunic (see Plate C1) was styled after the Army's 1842/95 _Waffenrock_, with a white standing collar and cuffs, blue "Brandenburg" cuff-flaps, white piping, and yellow double _Litzen_. Here it is mostly hidden by the M1867 enlisted ranks' black greatcoat, worn by the Seebataillone into World War I. (AdeQ HA)**

RIGHT **A new two-pocket, standing-collar khaki summer uniform was authorized for the III. Seebataillon in China on June 13, 1898, and was later issued to other marine detachments in China, Southwest Africa, East Africa, and at Skutari. A white tropical helmet was initially issued, bearing a white-metal eagle plate above a small cockade. The eagle plate changed to bronze from June 25, 1900, and in 1905 the helmet became khaki for enlisted ranks below senior NCO. (AdeQ HA)**

This NCO of the III. Seebataillon was photographed in Tsingtao, China, prior to World War I; the "swallow's-nests" on his shoulders identify him as a musician. By 1914 an M1900 gray *Litewka* had replaced this dark blue M1893 for winter service dress overseas. The M1900 differed not only in color but also in having plain cuffs and two buttoned skirt pockets; it retained the white collar with yellow double *Litzen*, and white shoulder straps. (AdeQ HA)

rebellions (1904–08), and two companies were shipped to East Africa during the Maji-Maji uprising (1905–07). In 1913, apart from the III. Seebataillon at Tsingtao and the East Asian Marine Detachment at Peking, Tientsin, and Kiautschou, a composite company drawn from the I. & II. Seebataillone (Marine Detachment Skutari, under Lt Paul Schneider) was serving with international occupation troops in Albania.[3]

* * *

The outbreak of the Great War brought the rapid expansion of marine forces. The I. & II. Seebataillone were each expanded into a Marine Regiment, and were deployed as the Naval Infantry Brigade (Gen von Wiechmann) at the far northern end of the Western Front on the Flanders coast of Belgium. Depot troops and the 10. Seebataillon (ex-Marine Detachment Skutari) formed the nucleus of a 3rd Marine Regt, and the term Seebataillon passed out of use. Drawing on reservists and conscripts, by the end of 1914 two Marine divisions had been created, forming Marinekorps Flandern under Adm Ludwig von Schröder.

These Seesoldaten in Flanders in 1917 wear a mixture of field-gray M1910 and M1915 tunics based on the Army models, but retain their traditional yellow collar *Litzen* and shoulder-strap insignia, and a white band and piping on their field-gray field caps. (AdeQ HA)

[3] See MAA 466, *Armies of the Balkan Wars 1912–13*

Formation of a third division in early February 1917 raised the naval infantry corps to a strength of 60,000–70,000 men. Marine units fought in 1914 at Antwerp, in 1915 at Ypres, in 1916 on the Somme, in 1917 in Flanders, and in 1918 against the Zeebrugge Raid in April and during the German spring offensive. The naval infantry arm ceased to exist after the Armistice of November 11, 1918 and the subsequent Treaty of Versailles in 1919.

WORLD WAR I OVERSEAS

When World War I broke out in August 1914, most German colonial governors had only meager garrisons and resources with which to face the threats from the usually much stronger colonial forces of the Entente powers.

Togo

An Allied surrender demand was refused on August 6, 1914, and British and French forces invaded on August 9. British troops captured Lomé and part of the coast without resistance on the 12th. German troops under Maj Hans-Georg von Döring withdrew on Kamina, site of their strategic radio station, and slowed the pursuit of Col Bryant's force by destroying railroad bridges. At the Chra River some 60 Germans and 500 Togolese askaris from the Cameroon Schutztruppe conducted a successful delaying action for two days, taking 13 casualties while

LEFT **General Berthold von Deimling (1853–1944) served in Southwest Africa before returning home to command a brigade of infantry in 1907. During World War I, he commanded troops during the battles of Mulhouse, Verdun, and the Somme. It is interesting that he chose to pose for this portrait in Schutztruppe uniform. The light stone-gray 1897 home-service pattern has added general officer's distinctions: gold embroidered oakleaves on a red collar and red cuffs, gold cords on his shoulder straps, and gold lace edging to the brim of his** *Südwesterhut.* **(AdeQ HA)**

RIGHT **Included for comparison purposes only, this is a portrait of a German gunner (probably of 701. Artillerie-Abteilung) serving in Palestine with the Asienkorps sent to assist the Ottoman Army in 1917. His arm-of-service is identified by a black cloth band, piped red, around his M1902 tropical helmet; this also shows a brass eagle plate on the front, a large Imperial cockade on the right side, and a sun curtain. Many German troops serving in the Middle East, Balkans, and Caucasus wore their field-gray uniforms, in this case the M1915** *Bluse***; however, many wore a similarly cut M1916 khaki cotton uniform, or a mixture of both, or even old stock left over from the Army's Chinese deployments in 1900–09. (AdeQ HA)**

inflicting 23 killed and 52 wounded on the British. On August 24 the Germans destroyed the Kamina radio station to prevent its capture, and Maj von Döring surrendered with his remaining 200 men three days later.

Cameroon

Three British columns that advanced into the north from Nigeria were defeated by a combination of difficult terrain and ambushes. The French attacked the south from Chad and captured Kusseri; and early in September 1914 a Franco-Belgian force from the Congo, in an improvised flotilla of small craft, captured Limbe on the coast with British and French naval gunfire support. The capital, Duala, fell on September 27. Inland, the British captured Garua in June 1915, leaving Yaoundé as the only major center in German hands. After waiting for the dry season, a Franco-Belgian force followed the railroad inland, beating off ambushes along the way, and captured the town in November 1915. Many surviving Schutztruppen withdrew into neutral Spanish Guinea, to be interned for the duration of the war. The last German fort at Mora surrendered in February 1916.

German Southwest Africa

South African troops from Cape Colony were repulsed at Sandfontein in an action that began on September 26, 1914. About 2,600 British and South African and 522 African troops, with 4x 13-pdr guns and 4,347 animals, badly needed to reach water when they were engaged and defeated from higher ground by some 1,700 Schutztruppe riflemen with 4 machine guns and 10 artillery pieces.

On February 4, 1915 a German attempt to capture the Kakamas fords over the Orange River to disrupt South African invasion plans was beaten back. On February 11 the Boer War veteran Gen Louis Botha arrived in the German coastal town of Swakopmund to take command of the northern of two invasion forces. This advanced along the Swakopmund–Windhoek railroad in March; it took Otjimbingwe, Karibib,

The 7.5cm L17/08 mountain gun was designed by Rheinmetall; only 12 guns were made, and the entire production was sent to Germany's African colonies. The gun could be dismantled into five loads for transport by pack animals, and could be fitted with a shield for the crew. A similar weapon surrendered at Khorab in Southwest Africa to Gen Botha's South African Union forces is currently in the collections of the Imperial War Museum, London.

After hostilities ended in East Africa the British transferred the German POWs to Dar es Salaam for repatriation, and Gen von Lettow-Vorbeck tried to ensure decent treatment and the briefest internment at Tabora for his askaris. As the commander of the only colonial force not to have been defeated in the field, he returned home in early March 1919 to a hero's welcome. He was given the unique privilege of leading 120 officers of the Schutztruppe, in their war-worn tropical uniforms, on a victory parade through the Brandenburg Gate, which was decorated in their honor. He is seen here astride his black charger; note the white band of German East Africa on his slouch hat. His men, returned from captivity, wore a mixture of German and British headgear and uniforms. Note in the foreground the extended rear profile of the 1902 Bortfeldt tropical helmet, official issue to the Schutztruppe from 1913. (AdeQ HA)

Friedrichsfelde, Wilhelmsthal, and Okahandja, and entered Windhoek with no resistance on May 5, 1915.

After rejecting the terms of a German offer to surrender, Gen Botha proceeded effectively to cut the colony in half by unleashing four columns: north to Outjo and the Etosha Pan; along the Swakopmund–Tsumeb railroad; and by more southerly routes, to Tsumeb and Otavi Junction. On July 1 the Schutztruppe in the northwest made a last stand at Otavi, and on July 9 their last commander, Victor Franke, surrendered near Khorab.

Meanwhile, the South African southern force under Gen Jan Smuts had landed at Lüderitz Bay. Advancing inland, he captured Keetmanshoop on May 20, 1915. There he linked with two other South African columns, and followed the railroad north to Berseba. He captured Gibeon on May 26 after two days' fighting; this obliged the remaining Schutztruppe in the south to retreat northward towards Windhoek, where Gen Botha was waiting. Within two weeks the German forces in the south capitulated.

German East Africa

Paul von Lettow-Vorbeck's conduct of by far the most impressive campaign in Germany's colonies would become legendary. Rather than summarize it inadequately here, we direct the reader to the detailed account in Peter Abbott's MAA 379, *Armies in East Africa 1914–18*. It is enough to note that the German commander, who started the war with just 2,600 German nationals and 2,472 African askaris, consistently outmaneuvered and tied down, and often outfought, British Empire and Allied forces many times stronger. With a command that never exceeded about 3,000 Germans and 12,000 Africans, for four years he held in check up to 300,000 British Empire, Belgian, and Portuguese troops. He still had 1,500 men under arms in British Northern Rhodesia when he finally agreed to a ceasefire, three days after the end of the war in Europe.

China

The garrison of Tsingtao consisted of the III. Seebataillon, naval personnel, Chinese colonial troops, and Austro-Hungarian sailors, for a total strength of 3,625 men under arms. There were also a torpedo boat and four small gunboats, as well as the Austro-Hungarian cruiser SMS *Kaiserin Elisabeth*, whose crew were initially divided to both man the ship and fight on land.

The threat came from Japan, which landed the first of some 23,000 troops on September 2, 1914 at Longkou, and on September 18 at Laoshan Bay about 18 miles east of Tsingtao. The primary formation was the 18th Infantry Division; however, the British and other Allied powers were concerned about Japanese intentions in the region, and London decided to send a largely symbolic 1,500-man contingent from Tientsin to represent their interests. This consisted of 1,000 soldiers of the 2nd Bn South Wales Borderers, later followed by 500 from the 36th Sikhs.

The Japanese began digging siege parallels, and commenced their bombardment on October 31. They had about 100 heavy guns, each with 1,200 rounds; by night the howitzers and the guns on their warships shelled the German defenses constantly, while the Japanese advanced their trenches. The garrison troops were able to reply to this seven-day bombardment with the heavy guns of the harbor fortifications, but soon ran short of ammunition. On the evening of November 6 the Japanese infantry attacked and overwhelmed the outer line of defenses. The next morning the German naval governor, Capt Alfred Meyer-Waldeck, asked for terms, and the Allies took formal possession of the colony on November 16, 1914.

Total German casualties were 199 dead and 504 wounded; Japanese casualties, 236 killed and 1,282 wounded; and British losses, 12 killed and 53 wounded. The German prisoners were shipped to camps in Japan, from which the last were not released until early 1920, but they reported that they had generally been treated well.

The Pacific

On the outbreak of war the British government requested that Australia and New Zealand send forces to capture or disable German radio stations on New Guinea's dependent islands, which supported the operations of Adm von Spee's German East Asian Cruiser Squadron.[4] An Australian force about 2,000 strong sailed from Sydney on September 7, 1914, and landed at Rabaul in New Pomerania on the 11th. Governor Eduard Haber had only a handful of native police and recalled German civilian reservists, but at first he refused a surrender demand in the hope of relief by Adm von Spee's warships. The only real action took place around the radio station at Bita Paka, where the Australians suffered a dozen casualties before the radio was captured in working order; the defenders lost one German and about 30 Melanesians killed and 11 wounded.

4 See MAA 473, *New Zealand Expeditionary Force in World War I*, and MAA 478, *Australian Army in World War I*.

The Polizeitruppe had a total strength of only 283 men scattered throughout the Micronesian archipelagos, and the Imperial Japanese Navy took all the German islands without opposition between September 29 and October 21, 1914. The only act of potential resistance was on Ponape, where a district officer named Koehler and two German police NCOs at first retreated into the bush with about 50 native policemen; they wisely surrendered after seeing the size of the Japanese landing force.

The German governor of Samoa, Dr Schultz-Erwerth, was under no illusions as to his ability to defend the colony. The few German civilians were not officially called up as reservists, but about 50 traders, planters, and officials formed a citizens' force known as the Bürgerwehr, to protect the radio station and act as coast guards. In the event they saw no action; when a 1,400-strong New Zealand force arrived with British and French warships off Apia on August 29, 1914, the governor quickly negotiated a surrender without a shot being fired.

AFTERMATH

Following the loss to the Allies of all Germany's overseas possessions, she was formally stripped of them by the Treaty of Versailles in 1919. In Africa, Togo was handed to France, which divided Cameroon with Britain; German Southwest Africa became part of the British Empire, and German East Africa was divided between Britain, Portugal, and Belgium. In the Pacific, Kaiser-Wilhelmsland and the Bismarck Archipelago – the bulk of German New Guinea – were awarded to Australia. The phosphate-rich island of Nauru came under joint administration by Britain, Australia, and New Zealand, and German Samoa was given to New Zealand. The islands north of the equator went to Japan, which also occupied Tsingtao in China.

German Colonial Veterans' Associations

The first of the colonial veterans' associations can be traced back to 1896, and an umbrella organization – the German Union of Veterans' Associations of Chinese and African Military Campaigns (Vereinigung der Kriegervereine ehemaliger China - und Afrikakrieger von Deutschland) – was established in Berlin in 1902. By the outbreak of the Great War nearly 110 separate local associations were registered.

The German Colonial Fighters' Union (Deutsche Kolonialkriegerbund, DKKB), headed by MajGen Georg Maercker, was established in 1922 to keep their traditions alive, and by 1926 some 80 associations

This former member of the Schutztruppe is wearing a brown corduroy replica of the piped campaign service uniform. As a member of a veterans' organization under the Third Reich, he is required to wear the Nazi Party armband; obscured here is the metal breast eagle of the German Veterans' League pinned above the right breast pocket. The shield-shaped badge on his left forearm, copied from the original *"Petersflagge"* of East Africa, was adopted after World War I as the traditional emblem of the German colonies: a black cross on white, with the seven white stars of the Southern Cross in the red first canton. This was also displayed by selected German police units that were chosen to preserve the lineage of the German colonial police forces. (AdeQ HA)

and 34 territorial groups existed. During the Third Reich the Imperial Colonial Union (Reichskolonialbund, RKB), headed by Franz Ritter von Epp, provided coordination; by 1942 it united about 12,000 colonial veterans in 120 separate associations nationwide. The RKB was dissolved on February 17, 1943, together with the Nazis' Office for Colonial Policy (Kolonialpolitisches Amt der NSDAP).

Eleven years after World War II, the Union of Former Colonial Troops (Verband ehemaliger Kolonialtruppen) was established in Hamburg on June 3, 1956. With the death of the last colonial veterans, in 1983 the organization modified its name to the Traditional Union of Former Colonial and Overseas Troops – Friends of the Former German Protectorates (Der Traditionsverband ehemaliger Schutz- und Überseetruppen – Freunde der früheren deutschen Schutzgebiete e. V.). This survives today as a historical society, dedicated to preserving the history and the sites relating to Germany's colonial past.

* * *

In 1964, the year of Paul von Lettow-Vorbeck's death, the West German parliament voted to deliver back pay to all surviving askaris, and a temporary cashier's office was set up at Mwanza on Lake Victoria. Of the 350 aged veterans who gathered, only a handful could produce the certificates that von Lettow-Vorbeck had given them in 1918, though others presented pieces of their old uniforms as proof of service. The German banker who had brought the money came up with an idea: as each claimant stepped forward, he was handed a broom and ordered in German to perform the manual of arms. Not one man failed the test.

Four barracks of the German Army (Bundeswehr) were once named in honor of Gen von Lettow-Vorbeck, but only one now remains: the Lettow-Vorbeck-Kaserne in Leer, East Frisia. Street names and monuments commemorating individuals, units, and campaigns relating to the former colonies are still encountered, and are still occasionally being erected, in various places in Germany. In Namibia and other former colonies, crumbling forts and other buildings are reminders to this day of the German colonial presence.

SELECT BIBLIOGRAPHY

anon, *Die Deutsche Schutztruppe für Südwest-Afrika* (Leipzig; Verlag von Moritz Ruhl, 1895)

anon, *Handbook of the German Army* (London; Imperial War Museum, 2002 – r/p of War Office 1912/amended 1914 edn)

anon, *Schutztruppen-Ordnung für die Kaiserlichen Truppen in Afrika, 1898/1908: Organisatorische Bestimmungen und Uniformierung* (Wolfenbüttel, Germany; Mechior Historischer Verlag, 2011)

Bassett-Powell, Bruce, *Imperial German Schutztruppe 1891–1914, Uniformology Book Series No. 6* (Weathersford, TX; Uniformology, 2006)

Collyer, J.J., *The Campaign in German South West Africa* (London; Imperial War Museum, 1997 – r/p of 1937 edn)

Collyer, J.J., *The South Africans with General Smuts in German East Africa* (London; Imperial War Museum, 2004 – r/p of 1939 edn)

de Quesada, Alejandro M., *Uniforms of the German Soldier: An Illustrated History from 1870 to the First World War* (London; Greenhill Books, 2006)

Dobbertin, Walther, *Lettow-Vorbeck's Soldiers: A Book of German Fighting Spirit and Military Honor* (Nashville, TN; The Battery Press, 2005 – r/p of 1932 edn)

Farwell, Byron, *The Great War in Africa* (New York; W.W. Norton & Co., 1986)

Gottschall, Terrell D., *By Order of the Kaiser: Otto von Diederichs and the Rise of the Imperial German Navy, 1865–1902* (Annapolis; Naval Institute Press, 2003)

Hoyt, Edwin P., *The Last Cruise of the Emden* (New York; Macmillan Co., 1966)

Lohse, Volker, "Die deutsche Polizeitruppe für Togo und andere Sicherungskräfte im Schutzgebiet (1885–1914)", in *Mitteilungsblatt von Traditionsverband ehemaliger Schutz- und Überseetruppen – Freunde der früheren deutschen Schutzgebiete e. V.*, Nr. 96 (December 2011), 5–62

Nigmann, Ernst, *German Schutztruppe in East Africa: History of the Imperial Protectoriate Force, 1889–1911* (Nashville, TN; Battery Press, 2005 – r/p of 1911 Ernst Siegfried Mittler & Sohne edn)

Pukariga, Dasana, "Dagbon: Recalling History, the Battle of Adibo" (www.dagbon.net/yela/Adibodali). This draws partly upon a lecture by Dr Peter Sebald, "From the Ewe Country to Dagomba – The German Occupation of 1888–1900," delivered at the Goethe Institute, Accra, Ghana, on January 11, 2005.

Sibley, J.R., *Tanganyikan Guerilla: East African Campaign 1914–18* (New York; Ballantine Books Inc., 1971)

Whitefield, D. George, "The Nicaragua Canal", in Foreign and Commonwealth Office Collection, 1892

Willmott, H.P., *First World War* (London; Dorling Kindersley, 2003)

Woolley, Charles, *Uniforms of the German Colonial Troops, 1884–1918* (Atglen, PA; Schiffer Military History, 2009)

Zimmerer, Jürgen & Joachim Zeller, *Genocide in German South-West Africa: The Colonial War of 1904–1908 and its Aftermath* (Monmouth, UK; Merlin Press Ltd, 2008)

For more detail about the Schutztruppe, see also the website of Der Traditionsverband ehemaliger Schutz- und Überseetruppen – Freunde der früheren deutschen Schutzgebiete e. V. at www.traditionsverband.de

Other informative online reference sites dealing with German colonial troops in English are, particularly, Chris Dale's www.GermanColonialUniforms.co.uk, and www.savageandsoldier.com/articles/africa/GermanWars, by Paul Beck, Nick Stern, & John Switzer

PLATE COMMENTARIES

A: GERMAN SOUTHWEST AFRICA SCHUTZTRUPPE, 1890s

A1: *Major*, *c*.1894–96

This *Käppi* was originally worn by all ranks of the Schutztruppe, before being replaced by the visored German field cap ordered in November 1896. It was in gray cloth, with a band in the identifying color of the colony (cornflower-blue for Southwest Africa, white for East Africa, or red for Cameroon); an officer's silver rank ring; and a small black/white/red Imperial cockade on the front. This khaki cotton uniform was authorized for officers from 1894 for use in hot weather as an alternative to the corduroy uniform (both corduroy and cotton uniforms had been used by the old Truppe des Reichs-Kommissars of 1888 onward). The original stand collar was replaced by this more comfortable stand-and-fall type; note two inwards-slanting pleated breast pockets, but no skirt pockets. Colony-color piping is seen around the collar and down the front, and cuff-edging in a pointed shape recalling the "Polish" cuffs of the corduroy uniform. Officer ranks in the Schutztruppe were distinguished on both the home and colonial uniforms by shoulder straps in the style of the Imperial Army, with backing in the relevant colony color. Junior officers' straps were of flat silver cords with "arrowheads" of black and red threads making a zigzag pattern, and senior officers' of interwoven cords, both with the appropriate "pips" of their rank. This major's belt and sword knot are silver with black and red lines, the gilt buckle bearing the Imperial crown. In the field a leather "Sam Browne"-style belt would commonly be worn, without a sword. The change to new uniform items from 1896 was gradual, and earlier and newer types may be seen side-by-side in photographs.

A2: *Reiter*, corduroy uniform, from 1896

In the all-European Southwest Africa force a mounted-infantry private was designated a Reiter or trooper. The 1896 *Südwesterhut* ("Southwestern Hat") was of gray felt with a band and brim-edging in colony color, the right side being pinned up with a large Imperial cockade. The earlier corduroy service uniform was modified in 1894 with the addition of collar and pointed "Polish" cuffs in the cornflower-blue of this colony, decorated with *Litzen*; for enlisted men these were single, white with a red central line, and for senior NCOs and officers double, of silver metallic braid. The enlisted ranks' shoulder straps were of white mohair cords with black and red "arrowhead" threads. The tunic had breast pockets only, and six white-metal front buttons

bearing, as always, the Imperial crown. The trouser outseams were initially piped in colony colors, but an order discontinuing this from December 29, 1913 may have been anticipated by some years. This mounted infantryman wears long leather gaiters over ankle boots, an alternative to riding boots. Before an order of January 27, 1894 the plaited-cord marksmanship lanyards worn across the right breast were in the state colors of the previous regiment in which they had been earned; thereafter they were awarded to Schutztruppen in the Imperial colors.

A3: *Trooper*, *Kord Waffenrock*, *c*.1897

This new corduroy tunic was ordered on November 19, 1896, both as a home uniform for wear in Germany, and as a cold-weather service uniform for Africa. Almost immediately, on March 11, 1897, another order replaced it for use in Germany with a new light gray home uniform of identical cut, but it was retained for service in Africa. The new corduroy *Waffenrock* had a stand-and-fall collar and straight "Swedish" cuffs in colony colors, retaining the *Litzen*. The tunic had no visible pockets, and was piped in colony colors down the front and around three-button rear pleats of scalloped shape, "*à la soubise*." There were eight front buttons, two on each cuff, and small ones fastening the shoulder straps. For enlisted ranks the strap design was unchanged; NCOs' distinctions continued to be silver braid edging to the collar and cuffs, and collar side-buttons as appropriate. This trooper wears the standard-issue Prussian dragoon riding boots, and the Schutztruppe brown belt and pouch mounted equipment, which buckled at the back. (At the same date officers were authorized a *Kord Interimstock*, cut like the *Waffenrock* but with plain corduroy collar and cuffs piped in colony colors.)

A4: *Unteroffizier*, *Kord Litewka*, *c*.1897

This corporal wears the visored field cap introduced on November 19, 1896 to replace the *Käppi* for all ranks. Made

Two soldiers of the Southwest Africa Schutztruppe afford an excellent view of the winter and summer field uniforms adopted on November 19, 1896.
(Left) The Reiter wears the gray felt slouch hat, with a band and brim-edging in that colony's cornflower-blue identifying color. His khaki *Kord Waffenrock* (see Plate A3) has a blue collar and Swedish cuffs with white *Litzen* (very extended on the collar). Just visible are knee-length strapped gaiters.
(Right) The Unteroffizier has the visored corduroy field cap, with band in colony color. With darker cord breeches, he wears the four-pocket khaki cotton tunic; this differed in being piped in blue round the collar and cuffs and down the front for service in all three African colonies. His left sleeve bears the single (removable) chevron of his rank, in silver on narrow blue backing; a Sergeant wore two chevrons, a Vize-Feldwebel three, and a Feldwebel four, though in the latter case the "concentric" arrangement made the upper chevron little more than a small central triangle. (AdeQ HA)

An NCO in the light gray 1897 home-service Tuchrock; the silver braid round his collar, but lack of a collar side-button, identifies the rank of Unteroffizier. The 1896 Südwesterhut was usually worn with the home uniform, with a band and brim-edging in colony color, and a large Imperial cockade holding up the right-hand side. The alternative headgear was a matching gray field cap, with band and crown-piping in colony color, a black leather visor, and a small Imperial cockade on the front. (AdeQ HA)

BELOW Officers wore the same stone-gray home uniform from 1897. It differed from that of the enlisted ranks only in quality and ornamentation, with large silver double *Litzen* covering more of the colony-colored collar. Junior officers' shoulder straps continued to be on colony-color backing, with flat silver cords interwoven with red and black "arrowhead" threads making a zigzag pattern, and one and two metal rank "pips" for Oberleutnant and Hauptmann respectively. The left-shoulder aiguillettes, here in silver cord, were not particular to officers; all ranks wore them for parade order, the enlisted ranks in Imperial-color cords. (AdeQ HA)

of corduroy, it had a colony-colored band, a black visor, and sometimes a black chinstrap. (A light gray cloth version from the 1897 home-service uniform was sometimes seen in Africa.) New cold- and hot-weather field uniforms were introduced by the same orders; again, the changeover took time, and different patterns might be seen together for several years. This cold-weather *Kord Litewka* was exclusive to Southwest Africa, and might be worn by all ranks. It had a plain corduroy stand-and-fall collar and plain cuffs, a fly front, and no colored piping. Four internal pockets had slightly inward-slanting flaps on the breast and level flaps on the skirt, with concealed buttons. The only visible buttons were a pair in the small of the back to support a belt, and those on the unchanged shoulder straps. On this uniform NCOs were distinguished by large silver chevrons on the upper left sleeve. Orders of December 29, 1913 definitively replaced the *Waffenrock* with this garment, which was then renamed the *Kord Feldrock*. It is unclear how widely this order was obeyed during the eight months before the outbreak of war cut the colony's lines of supply.

The contemporary November 1896 hot-weather uniform was of khaki cotton, with six front buttons, a plain collar and cuffs, pleated breast pockets with inward-slanting buttoned flaps, and unpleated skirt pockets with level buttoned flaps. Uniquely, it was piped on the collar, front, and cuffs in blue for all colonies. Again, NCO chevrons were worn on the left sleeve.

B: CHINA, 1900–14

B1: *Soldat*, 1st (Prussian) Regiment, East Asian Expeditionary Corps, 1900–01

This cyclist-infantryman wears the straw hat (*Strohut*) designed for service in China. Similar in shape to the Schutztruppe *Südwester*, it had a narrow band in company color (1st Co white, 2nd red, 3rd yellow, and 4th blue). A large Imperial cockade surmounted a smaller one in Prussian, Bavarian, Saxon, Württemberg, or Baden state colors. On August 12, 1900 this unpopular hat was ordered replaced with a plain khaki *Bordmütze* field cap with a gray leather visor, and in December 1900 with the Navy's 1895-pattern Bortfeldt tropical helmet, in khaki complete with a hook-on sun curtain. The khaki cotton

sometimes wore the khaki tunic with home-service breeches. Since the Expeditionary Corps was formed from the best volunteers, large numbers of marksmanship lanyards are seen in photos. The black leather equipment has 1895 pouches, and the rifle is the *Gewehr 98*.

B2: *Polizei-Soldat*, Tsingtau Polizeitruppe, 1909–14

In 1909 the remainder of the Chinese Company of the III. Seebatallion was absorbed into the Tsingtao Police, which was also led by cadres from that battalion or from the Navy artillery batteries. (The East Asian Expeditionary Corps/Occupation Brigade also employed Chinese troops, until these were disbanded when their parent units were repatriated between 1901 and 1909.) This mounted policeman is dressed in the dark blue-gray padded winter uniform, with a matching turban, and riding boots; puttees or fur-lined Chinese boots were also seen. He carries a German M1889 cavalry sabre without a sword knot; dismounted police usually carried truncheons, but were issued rifles at need. Each man had a left-sleeve patch with his individual service number in both Western and Chinese characters. Obscured here is the long traditional pigtail, which was worn tucked into the belt at the back.

B3: *Kanonier*, 1st East Asian Field Artillery Battalion, East Asian Occupation Brigade, 1901–09

Over the turn of 1900–01, new winter and summer uniforms were ordered, item by item, and consolidated by orders of February 9, 1901. They were of similar cut, but in light field-gray and khaki respectively. This "1900" *Rockbluse* had a stand-and-fall collar; four pockets with concealed buttons, the breast flaps slightly slanted; plain cuffs (turn-back on the winter uniform); a fly front, and three-button scalloped rear skirt pleats. The collar, front, cuffs, and rear pleats were piped red. Shoulder straps were in arm-of-service color, so here red with a yellow flaming-shell badge; plain straps piped in the arm color are also seen in photos. NCOs wore white/red/black lace around the collar (with the appropriate side-buttons), around the cuffs, and in a single left-sleeve chevron. Matching trousers were piped red on the outseams, but breeches were not. Field caps were, for winter, field-gray with red piping and a band in arm-of-service color, and for summer plain khaki with a button-on sun curtain; visors were gray and chinstraps brown. The M1902 Bortfeldt tropical helmet (see C2) was worn for summer service. New ammunition pouches resembled the M1909 but in gray leather, and were worn individually in

Drillichrock tunic, with a standing collar, was an adaptation of the Army's *Drilljacke* fatigue jacket. Here it has one left breast pocket, six brass front buttons, and a plain cuff, but state variations were seen. There were two waist buttons on the plain rear, and two buttoned belt-support loops. In winter these white shoulder straps with red regimental number were worn on the Army's blue home-service *Litewka*. NCOs wore a strip of white lace heavily interwoven with wide red and narrow black lines round the top and front edges of the collar, and side-buttons as appropriate. Matching trousers were issued but not breeches, so mounted men

This infantryman of the East Asian Occupation Brigade, 1901–09, wears the winter uniform: a light field-gray wool *Litewka* with red piping on the collar, fly front, cuffs, and rear skirts – see Plate B3. Only the white piping on his shoulder straps identifies the tunic to the infantry arm. The summer field cap was plain khaki; the field-gray winter version was piped red round the crown, with a band in the arm-of-service color. (AdeQ HA)

threes or twos rather than being made in one-piece sets.

In winter walking-out dress, this gunner from the 1. Ostasiatische Feld Artillerie Abteilung wears the new uniform with the M1900 ball-topped artillery *Kugelhelm* in gray pressed felt with leather visors front and rear, an eagle plate, and an Imperial cockade on the right – state distinctions disappeared with the creation of the Occupation Brigade. His carbine bayonet is hidden behind his hip; note his 1901 China Campaign Medal. In 1905 a new field-gray summer uniform replaced the khaki, but differed from this tunic in having pleated breast pockets with pointed flaps.

C: *SEEBATAILLONE*, 1900–18

C1: *Seesoldat, I. Seebataillon*; Kiel, c.1900

This marine wears the enlisted ranks' M1893 dark blue *Litewka* with white summer trousers; winter trousers were dark blue with white piping. The tunic has a white collar and cuffs and blue Brandenburg cuff-flaps; it is piped in white, including the three-button rear skirt pleats, and bears golden-yellow double *Litzen* on the collar and the cuff-flaps. The white shoulder straps display yellow insignia: an Imperial crown, above crossed anchors, above a small Roman battalion number. The peakless field cap was blue with a white band and piping, but rankers were permitted to buy privately this stiffened, visored NCO type for walking-out. He carries his black leather Jäger-style shako, with an oval Imperial cockade, above a brass eagle-and-anchor plate; unlike the Jägers, the sea-soldiers displayed no cockades round the chinstrap buttons.

C2: *Sergeant, III. Seebataillon*; Tsingtao, 1914

A khaki tropical uniform was ordered for this unit slightly earlier than for the Army, on June 13, 1898; it was later worn by other marine detachments overseas. (Photos show examples of blue and khaki uniform items being worn mixed together, and senior NCOs and officers wearing white and khaki mixed.) It had a stand-and-fall collar, six front buttons, two skirt pockets with buttoned flaps, plain cuffs and rear, and shoulder straps as for C1. The NCO lace round the cuffs and collar was the same as on Army khaki tunics, but collar rank buttons were worn forward rather than level with the shoulder strap. In 1898 the tropical helmet was white, with a white-metal plate worn above an Imperial cockade; the plate became bronze from June 28, 1900. Helmets officially became khaki for privates and junior NCOs during 1905, though photos show khaki or khaki-covered examples as early as 1900. The Bortfeldt 1902 tropical helmet, issued in 1904–05 to marines in SW Africa and to this battalion in China, differed from the first type in that its long rear brim could be folded upward at a slant, but obviously not when the sun curtain was hooked on. The rifle is the *Gewehr 98*; the leather equipment, with 1895 pouches, was first issued blackened but later left brown. This uniform soon wore out when used by marines in the Herero campaign, and was replaced with Schutztruppe issue, often including their slouch hat and back-buckling leather equipment.

C3: *Seesoldat, 1. Marine Division*; Belgium, 1917–18

The naval infantry in Flanders began the war in their blue home-service uniform, and although the Army-style field-gray M1910 uniform was authorized on September 4, 1914, it was slow to arrive; the blues were not officially discontinued until March 1, 1915. Although authorized on June 10, 1916, this M1915 *Bluse* did not appear until 1917; some group photos show M1910, M1910 modified, and M1915 jackets all being worn together. The marine units retained the yellow *Litzen* on the collar, but white piping only on the gray shoulder straps (with yellow insignia). The gray *Feldmütze* had a white band and crown-piping, though the former was often concealed with a gray strip. While this man wears the M1916 steel helmet, he still has the old M1895 pouches in blackened leather.

D: GERMAN EAST AFRICA *SCHUTZTRUPPE*, 1914–19

D1: *Soldat*, home uniform with overcoat, 1914

The light gray "*Tuchuniform*" was authorized on March 11, 1897 for wear in Germany by the Schutztruppe of all colonies and as a parade dress in Southwest Africa. Pocketless, it had eight white-metal buttons on the front and two on each "Swedish" cuff; a stand-and-fall collar and turnback cuffs in colony colors, with white or silver *Litzen*; and colony-color piping on the front edge and three-button rear pleats. Noncombatant officials such as doctors, paymasters, and gunsmiths wore the same uniform but with distinctive colors for their arms of service. This trooper wears it with breeches and riding boots, but it is almost hidden by the long Prussian single-breasted cavalry *Mantel*. This riding greatcoat had six front buttons, a deep collar and cuffs, slanted side pockets with buttoned flaps, and at the rear a deep central vent and a single-button cloth half-belt for size adjustment. On November 19, 1896 colony-colored shoulder straps and collar patches were authorized (blue collar patches had been worn in SW Africa since at least 1894). On November 28, 1899 *Litzen* were authorized on the collar patches.

D2: *Oberstleutnant* Paul Emil von Lettow-Vorbeck, 1915

Lieutenant-Colonel von Lettow-Vorbeck is wearing the field uniform for Schutztruppe officers that followed the European enlisted ranks' 1896 khaki summer dress in having the collar, front, cuffs, and trousers piped cornflower-blue. This uniform was authorized for use in all the African colonies, so the only East African feature illustrated is the white backing to his shoulder straps. As the war in East Africa dragged on, with von Lettow-Vorbeck's greatly expanded command cut off from resupply, the appearance of European officers and men became increasingly motley, with much use of civilian, improvised, and captured Allied items.

D3: *Askari* bugler of a *Feldkompagnie*, 1914

The askari headgear was the *tarbush*, made on a light wicker frame with a khaki cloth cover incorporating a neck curtain, the latter sometimes being rolled up. From 1896 a white-metal Imperial eagle badge was authorized; prior to this, metal Feldkompagnie numbers were occasionally seen, but usually no insignia at all. The light khaki uniform comprised a pocketless five-button tunic with plain stand-and-fall collar and shoulder straps, matching trousers to below the knee, puttees, and boots. Musicians were distinguished by "swallow's-nests" in khaki and red. In combat, musicians either fought as riflemen or acted as stretcher-bearers. In this latter role they wore either a white left armband with a red Geneva cross, or a white circular patch with a red cross sewn to the upper left sleeve. Note the old 1895 ammunition pouches; only a minority of the East African Schutztruppe had received the *Gewehr 98* by 1914, and further supplies depended upon infrequent blockade-runners.

D4: Returned prisoner of war; Berlin, 1919

This veteran soldier of Gen von Lettow-Vorbeck's command, returned after a few months in a South African prison camp, is partly dressed in castoff and modified British uniform items, but he retains an East Africa Schutztruppe gray field cap, his Iron Cross 1st Class, and on his left breast a fold of Colonial Campaign Medal ribbon.

E: COLONIAL AUXILIARY TROOPS, 1914–18

E1: Reservist of a *Schützenkompagnie*; German East Africa, 1914–18

As well as virtually doubling the number of his Schutztruppe field companies, by March 1915 Col von Lettow-Vorbeck had raised nine "sharpshooter companies" from European reservists and volunteers (Schützenkompagnien – the *umlaut* changes the meaning). They varied widely in numbers and quality; some were good only for garrison work, but some (e.g. the 8th and 9th) were first-class mounted infantry who served with his maneuver forces. This reservist wears a khaki tropical helmet (apparently the M1902, officially issued to the Schutztruppe in 1913), with a puggaree wrapped round it and the eagle badge from an askari's *tarbush* pinned above a small Imperial cockade. His pocketless tunic and brown leather belt with a plain brass buckle seem to be of the types usually issued to Schutztruppe askaris; his riding gaiters are typical of European colonial dress. Small strips of cloth in the Imperial colors have been slipped round his shoulder straps, and he has been issued an 11mm Mauser M1871/84 rifle.

E2: Reservist, German New Guinea, 1914

In an attempt to achieve a more-or-less uniform appearance

these reservists wore a variety of khaki clothing and slouch hats, identifying themselves with green brassards (the official colony color since 1912) round both arms, and/or a hat cockade. Equipment usually consisted of one 1909 (as here) or 1895 ammunition pouch on a leather belt with a Navy buckle, as also worn by the Polizeitruppe on New Guinea.

E3: Volunteer, *Bürgerwehr*; Samoa, 1914

This Citizens' Force assembled briefly from planters, traders, and officials in Samoa wore khaki clothing and some form of slouch hat. Like most reservists, he is carrying obsolete equipment: an M1871/84 rifle, with a single M1874 ammunition pouch hung below his Navy enlisted ranks' belt buckle.

E4: Reservist, Cameroon, 1914

He wears the same type of helmet as E1, again with the eagle badge from an askari's headgear, and a pocketless, four-button askari jacket with collar and cuff edging in the red identifying color of this colony (see Plate F4). He has added a brassard in national colors, to underline the fact that he is a legitimate combatant. Although he has makeshift equipment – one or more old 1895 cartridge pouches on a Schutztruppe German ranker's belt, supported apparently by the straps from bread-bags – he is lucky enough to be armed with an up-to-date 7.92mm Kar 98a, as issued to most German personnel of the Cameroon Schutztruppe.

F: NATIVE COLONIAL TROOPS

F1: *Polizei-Gefreiter*, Kaiser-Wilhelmsland, c.1910

This Melanesian soldier of the Polizeitruppe in mainland German New Guinea is wearing a khaki naval-style uniform and a field cap, both trimmed with red. The single left-sleeve chevron is that of a senior private.

F2: *Polizei-Soldat*, Micronesian islands, c.1910

This soldier from the Miokesen-Polizeitruppe, perhaps stationed in the Carolines, wears a white naval-style blouse (which was also worn with white or khaki three-quarter trousers as a fatigue uniform by the Cameroon Schutztruppe). It had three-quarter sleeves, and blue tape around the squared neck and in three bands across the chest, but bore no insignia. Like the Melanesian police (F1), these soldiers were also issued a khaki visored cap with red trim and a small Imperial cockade, and a dark red *sarong*. A more practical headgear was a large straw hat with the brim pinned up with a large cockade (normally on the right, but at least one photo shows the hat being worn back to front). Leather equipment was usually a brown belt with a Navy enlisted man's buckle, with or without 1895 pouches, but on occasion they were issued fuller marching gear. The usual weapon was the Mauser M1871 rifle with bayonet, but some later Mauser carbines were also issued.

F3: *Polizei-Soldat*, Togo, c.1912

From about 1910, a dark khaki visored field cap with red trim began to replace the 1891 "rolled" fez (see F4, but for the police with a brass eagle badge), although some of the Togo Polizeitruppe may have retained the fez until 1914. The 1894

This cheerful farewell group of Schutztruppe soldiers wear the long and voluminous cavalry-model *Mantel* or riding greatcoat – see Plate D1. The coat was stone-gray, with collar patches and shoulder straps in the appropriate colony color. Officers' coats differed, appearing in several variations, but were usually recognizable by a double row of buttons and officers' shoulder straps of rank. (AdeQ HA)

pocketless khaki uniform was similar to that worn by Schutztruppe askaris in Cameroon and East Africa, but with five or six brass buttons, and without khaki shoulder straps. For the Togo police it had a red stand collar, edged – like the cuffs – with yellow lace (the colony color, adopted in 1912). The tunic was tucked into below-knee-length trousers, under a red waist sash worn beneath the equipment – here with old M1874/87 pouches. Puttees and boots were worn only rarely.

F4: Sergeant, Cameroon *Schutztruppe*, c.1912
He wears the red 1891 "rolled" or "squashed" fez peculiar to West Africa, with a dark blue tassel and a white-metal eagle badge. The pocketless khaki tunic, with four or five white-metal front buttons and khaki shoulder straps, was introduced around 1900; note the red collar-edging and lace bar, and pointed cuff-edging. The matching trousers are worn with blue/gray puttees and brown ankle boots, though some soldiers went barefoot. His weapon is the Kar 98a carbine; he still has old M1895 pouches, but by 1914 Cameroon askaris had received M1909 equipment in brown leather. His light marching order includes a rolled blanket or tent section; a bread-bag on his back, and a canteen looped to his belt, are obscured here. Note that askaris had no rank of Vize-Feldwebel, and their one to four red chevrons on the left sleeve identified Gefreiter, Unteroffizier, Sergeant (at that date a German rank), and Feldwebel. In West Africa the native NCOs did not use the Turkish-style rank titles handed down in East Africa from the original Sudanese recruits. Uniquely in Cameroon, an African Feldwebel wore the blue-piped, four-pocket khaki 1896 tunic of German Schutztruppe personnel.

G: COLONIAL POLICE FORCES
G1: Ombascha, Polizeitruppe; German East Africa
This African senior private, known by the traditional Turkish rank equivalent to a Gefreiter, wears the uniform used between 1896 and 1914. On duty his khaki *tarbush* would bear a larger eagle badge than that of Schutztruppe askaris (see H2), and in yellow metal, but here he has the red Muslim fez usually worn when off-duty. The pocketless light khaki uniform, resembling that of the Schutztruppe, has an oval red-on-white "P" (for Polizei) patch above his single red rank chevron.

G2: Wachmeister, Landespolizei; German Southwest Africa, 1905–09
This German senior NCO wears a tunic in the 1896 Schutztruppe style but in a distinctive darker khaki-brown. It has six brass front buttons; buttoned, pointed-flap, pleated breast pockets and plain skirt pockets; green shoulder straps, and a green stand-and-fall collar. Landespolizei rank insignia were worn in the form of lace on the shoulder straps, "pips" on the collar, and (though often omitted) green cuff-lace, the top stripe having a loop. Riding breeches were in brown or a lighter shade of corduroy or twill. The brown felt slouch hat had a band in paler khaki with a small Imperial cockade at the front, and the brim pinned up with a brass Imperial crown badge. The removable pouches on the bandolier belt carried ammunition for one of the variety of rifles and carbines used by this force; the sidearm was usually the 1883 *Reichsrevolver*. From 1905, sergeants and upward could carry a sword resembling the Prussian light cavalry saber, though not on active service after June 24, 1909.

Africans did serve as police auxiliaries in this colony, wearing standard Schutztruppe uniforms but stripped of the collar and cuff *Litzen* and shoulder straps, and identified by a red waist sash worn under the belt equipment. From 1907 onward they began to be issued with standard German Landespolizei uniforms, with a white-on-red "LP" armband in place of the sash. On the outbreak of the Great War most of the police were incorporated into the Schutztruppe, whose uniform they then received.

G3: NCO, Fita Fita ceremonial guard; Samoa, 1910
The white uniform trimmed with blue consisted of a collarless tunic, sarong (*lava lava*), and visorless field cap with a small Imperial cockade; NCOs wore a visored cap, and had two blue cuff-stripes. An example of this Samoan ceremonial sash can be seen at the Imperial War Museum, London.

G4: Oberwachmeister, Polizeitruppe; Togo, c.1910
A white tropical tunic, based on the Schutztruppe 1896 type but without the latter's blue piping, became the norm for police officers and senior NCOs in all the colonies from the mid-1890s. His white peaked cap has a black leather visor, a red band and piping, and the usual small cockade. An alternative was a white tropical helmet with a brass eagle above a small Imperial cockade, and a silver/red/black twist cord around the base. On active service a khaki version of this uniform, or a mixture of white and khaki items, were often seen. This police rank was equivalent to Feldwebel (sergeant-major); in the Togo police, uniquely, the rank chevrons were worn on both sleeves. In 1912 yellow was authorized as the facing color for Togo, but probably did not widely replace the red before World War I.

H: INSIGNIA & DECORATIONS
The following plates were used on the *Pickelhaube*, tropical pith helmet, shako, and other headgear by German colonial and overseas personnel:
(1) *Pickelhaube* plate for East Asian Expeditionary Corps.
(2) *Tarbush* badge used by African askaris in Togo, Cameroon, and East Africa.
(3) Shako and tropical helmet plate of the *Seebataillone*.
(4) *Pickelhaube* plate of German Colonial Office officials.
(5) Belt plate used by German colonial and marine troops.

Medals and orders specific to colonial service:
(6) 1900–01 China Campaign Medal, awarded to German combatants and noncombatants during the Boxer Rebellion.
(7) 1904–08 Southwest Africa Campaign Medal, awarded to all Germans who had served in that colony during the Herero and Nama rebellions.
(8) Colonial Service Medal, awarded to all German combatants of the Imperial armed forces who had served in colonial and overseas campaigns.
(9) Elephant Order, instituted by Minister for Reconstruction in 1921 for all veterans of active service in the colonies during 1914–18.
(10) Lion Order, instituted by the German Colonial Veterans League (Deutschen Kolonialkriegerbund) in 1922. Two versions existed: in silver (for all veterans of the colonial and overseas troops) and bronze (for those who had done valuable work for the colonies at home).

INDEX

Illustrations are indicated in **bold**. Plates are indicated by letter, followed by page number and caption locator in brackets.